MUSLIMS IN AMERICA

MUSLIMS IN AMERICA

A Short History

EDWARD E. CURTIS IV

2009

OXFORD

UNIVERSITY PRESS

Oxford University Press, Inc., publishes works that further
Oxford University's objective of excellence
in research, scholarship, and education.

Oxford   New York
Auckland   Cape Town   Dar es Salaam   Hong Kong   Karachi
Kuala Lumpur   Madrid   Melbourne   Mexico City   Nairobi
New Delhi   Shanghai   Taipei   Toronto

With offices in
Argentina   Austria   Brazil   Chile   Czech Republic   France   Greece
Guatemala   Hungary   Italy   Japan   Poland   Portugal   Singapore
South Korea   Switzerland   Thailand   Turkey   Ukraine   Vietnam

Published by Oxford University Press, Inc.
198 Madison Avenue, New York, NY 10016

www.oup.com

Library of Congress Cataloging-in-Publication Data
Curtis, Edward E., 1970–
Muslims in America / Edward E. Curtis IV.
p.   cm.
Includes bibliographical references and index.
ISBN 978-0-19-536756-0
1. Muslims–United States–History.   2. Muslims–United States–Social conditions.
3. Islam–United States–History.   4. United States–Ethnic relations.
5. United States–Religious life and customs.   I. Title.
E184.M88C877 2009
305.6'970973—dc22   2008047566

Frontispiece: Maryam Khan, a Pakistani American engineer, outside
the Rabia-e-Balkhi Women's Hospital in Kabul, Afghanistan, 2005.

9 8 7 6

Printed in the United States of America
on acid-free paper

For my son, Zayd

CONTENTS

PREFACE
ix

CHAPTER ONE   Across the Black Atlantic:
The First Muslims in North America
1

CHAPTER TWO   The First American Converts to Islam
25

CHAPTER THREE   Twentieth-Century Muslim Immigrants:
From the Melting Pot to the Cold War
47

CHAPTER FOUR   Religious Awakenings of the Late
Twentieth Century
72

CHAPTER FIVE   Muslim Americans after 9/11
97

CHRONOLOGY
119

FURTHER READING
123

INDEX
129

PREFACE

O people! We created you from the same male and female, and made you distinct peoples and tribes so that you may know one another. The noblest among you in the sight of God is the most righteous.
—*Qur'an 49:13*

In 2007, one of my neighbors organized public protests against the inclusion of foot baths at the new terminal of the Indianapolis International Airport. These foot baths had been proposed on behalf of the hundred-plus African Muslim cabbies who regularly washed their feet before performing their daily prayers. Airport planning officials explained that it was a matter of public health. Without the foot baths, these cabdrivers would wash their feet in the hand sinks or use empty soda bottles to wash them outdoors in the cold. The cost of installing the two stainless steel basins would be less than $2,000, a token amount given that the new airport terminal budget was over $1 billion. The money would come from airline-generated revenues, not taxes.

My neighbor, a Baptist preacher, declared that such accommodation of the Muslim cabdrivers was "fraternization with the enemy" during a time of war, as he told a reporter from the *Indianapolis Star*. The minister had tragically lost a son in the Iraq war, although he insisted that his son's death was not the reason for his opposition to Muslims. Instead, he told a conservative website, he opposed the addition of the sinks on the basis that this was a first step toward "Islam's desired goal, which is to thrust the entire world under one single Islamic caliphate under sharia law."

When my neighbor staged a "citizens' rally" against the foot baths, the local media covered the affair. The Rev. Dr. Henry Gerner, a local leader of Christians for Peace and Justice in the Middle East, staged a counterprotest. He held a sign in his hand and stood outside the preacher's church. One churchgoer attempted to force the sign out of Gerner's hand, but Gerner, whose long white beard and kindly voice invited constant comparisons to Santa Claus, would not yield the sign. As the hand-to-hand struggle ensued, Gerner eventually fell to the ground—and an Indianapolis television station caught it all on tape.

Weeks later, my neighbor, the Baptist preacher who opposed the foot baths, appeared at my doorstep with his wife. It was Christmas time, and he handed us a festive tin of fudge and cookies along with a greeting card. My wife and I thanked them and, trying to be polite, invited them in. They declined.

If they had come into the house, they would have been surprised, probably shocked. We had just finished our Saturday lunch of stuffed grape leaves, chick pea dip, and tabbouli, and had moved to the basement to drink tea. Our lunch guests that day were all Muslims, a family of five. The dad was a Syrian, the mother a Moroccan, and the three young kids were Americans. I wonder what this pastor might have said—or felt—if he had met these really cute kids and their friendly parents. The sad truth is that even if he had met our guests, his deep prejudices might have prevented him from really seeing them, much less really knowing them.

But I hope that I am wrong. Indeed, I have written this book so that non-Muslim Americans may come to understand Muslim Americans just a little bit better. That purpose is captured by the epigraph of this preface, which I have taken from chapter 49, verse 13 of the Qur'an, a verse that is well-known among Muslims. In it, God speaks directly to human beings, proclaiming that humankind was created from a single pair of male and female and made into different peoples and ethnicities so that they might come to know each other.

There is a second meaning that I wish to communicate in quoting this verse of the Qur'an. Because Muslim America, like the rest of the country, is often divided along lines of race, class, and ethnicity, and because Muslim Americans have had such different life experiences, they often know very little about one another. Recently, I was speaking with a prominent Muslim philanthropist who is a first-generation immigrant from the Middle East. Although very well informed about a variety of topics, this man had no idea that there were practicing African American Muslims in his city before the 1960s. And what he did have to say about black Muslims in his town was not very complimentary.

This lack of knowledge about Muslim American history among Muslim Americans themselves is explained partly by the fact that many Muslim American leaders are first-generation immigrants without a collective memory of Islam in the United States. Many of these first-generation Muslim immigrants also lack deep and meaningful social ties to African American Muslims, among whom Islam first developed as a religious "denomination" that was national in scope. The incredible influx of Muslim immigrants after 1965 coincided with increasing patterns of racial segregation in the United States, and this racial segregation profoundly shaped contemporary Muslim American communities.

Since 1970, neighborhoods and schools have become more racially segregated in the United States. Most post-1965 Muslim immigrants, both richer and better educated than the average American, joined whites in taking flight from the inner city to the suburbs. Although Muslim Americans condemn racial discrimination and prejudice, they live, like most Americans, in a nation that is divided by race. These racial divisions and other social fissures mean that Muslim Americans, like most Americans, do not necessarily have close friendships, go to school, work, or pray with Muslims of a different race.

And yet, indigenous and immigrant Muslims have still influenced one another across the racial and other social lines that have divided them. They have shared ideas, disagreed with each other, and exchanged food, clothes, and other goods. Unearthing the history of Muslims in the United States means showing how Middle Eastern, South Asian, European, African, black, white, Hispanic, and other Muslim Americans have come in contact and sometimes in conflict with one another.

Telling the story of Muslim America also means tracing the connections of Muslim Americans to Muslims abroad. American Islam is a drama that has unfolded on a global stage marked by international crossings. Few know about the Muslim American slave Job Ben Solomon, who traveled from his native West Africa to North America, then from America to England, and finally back to his African home—all decades before the American Revolution. His global trek illustrates an important theme in the history of Muslim Americans.

Islam in America has been international and cross-cultural from its very beginning. Like most Americans in the New

World, Muslim Americans have never known a world that was not affected by contact, exchange, and confrontation across racial, ethnic, social, and geographic boundaries. The history of Muslims in the United States is at least in part a story about what happens when the lives of Muslims from various places collide with one another in a new, multicultural nation.

This book also explains how larger events in U.S. history have had an important impact on Muslim American life. It illustrates how the transatlantic slave trade resulted in the first major (and forced) migration of Muslims to the Americas, and how internal migrations of African Americans from the South to the North set the stage for African American conversion to Islam. This volume reveals how the National Origins Act of 1924 and the 1965 law that repealed it changed Muslim American life. It also explores how U.S. foreign policy affected Muslim American consciousness during the Cold War, and how the revival of Islam in the 1970s around the globe influenced the Islamic awakening in the United States. Finally, it surveys the impact of 9/11 on Muslim Americans.

In offering a religious history of Muslim America, this book rather blatantly avoids any extended analysis of terrorism. With only a very few exceptions, Muslim Americans are not and never have been terrorists. Focusing on the supposed Muslim "enemy" inside America may stir fear and sell books, but it does not accurately or fairly portray the mundane realities of Muslim American life. Islamophobia, or the irrational fear of Muslims, is a form of prejudice akin to racism and anti-Semitism that should be resisted. Avoiding Islamophobia, however, does not mean ducking difficult issues, and this book offers a sober and well-rounded portrait of socially conservative and politically active Muslim Americans—the people who are sometimes mistaken for violent radicals. The book also explores the lives of Muslim Americans who want nothing to do with politics and choose to focus instead on spiritual enlightenment or their family's financial success.

On the whole, this book illustrates how the saga of Muslim America is an inextricable part of the American story. In a time when some people see a contradiction between being Muslim and being American, the lives of the human beings narrated here cry out for recognition. Their simultaneously Muslim and American voices demand our respect, whether we are Muslim or not.

March 2009
Indianapolis, Indiana

CHAPTER ONE

Across the Black Atlantic: The First Muslims in North America

In 1730 or 1731, Ayuba Suleiman Diallo was enslaved near the Gambia River in Bundu, in the eastern part of what is now the West African nation of Senegal. A slave ship carried this father and husband across the Atlantic Ocean to Annapolis, Maryland, where he was sold to a tobacco farmer. In America, Ayuba, who was named after the biblical figure and qur'anic prophet Job, became known by a translation of his name, Job Ben Solomon, or Job, the son of Solomon. He toiled in the tobacco fields, but soon fell ill and complained that he was not suited for such work. His owner allowed him to tend the cattle instead. These lighter duties allowed Job, who was a practicing Muslim, to maintain his daily prayer schedule, and he would often walk into the woods to pray. Job's peaceful devotions were soon disturbed, however, by a young white boy who mocked him and even threw dirt on him—and did so more than once. Perhaps for this reason, Job decided in 1731 to escape his bondage and head west. When a local jailer caught him, Job tried to explain why he had run away but he

1

was unable to communicate in English. Eventually, an African translator was found, and when Job was returned to the plantation, his owner set aside a place where Job could pray without disturbance.

But Job had a plan to escape his enslavement in America, and he wrote a letter in Arabic to his father, a prominent person, probably a religious scholar, in Bundu, hoping that his father might ransom him. Like other educated Muslims of the Fulbe or Fulani ethnic group, Job spoke Fula in daily life, but he could also read and write Arabic, a common West African language of learning, statecraft, and commerce in the eighteenth century. As a Muslim child, Job had memorized the Qur'an and studied numerous religious texts and traditions in Arabic.

Such knowledge impressed many of the white people whom Job met in his global travels. One of them was James Oglethorpe, the founder of Georgia and a member of the British parliament. Though Job's father never received the Arabic letter, Oglethorpe eventually came into possession of it and asked scholars at Oxford University to translate the letter into English. Oglethorpe, impressed by the slave's literacy and sympathetic to his story, then purchased his "bond." With Oglethorpe's assistance, Job crossed the Atlantic again, just two years or so after he had arrived in Annapolis. This time, he traveled to England. During this 1733 sea voyage, his biographer, the Rev. Thomas Bluett, noted that Job often prayed; butchered his own meat according to the rules outlined in the *shari'a*, or Islamic law and ethics; and avoided all pork.

During his stay in England, Job was said to have written in his own hand three complete copies of the Qur'an—from memory. Some of his sponsors had hoped to convert him to Christianity, and they gave him a copy of the New Testament in Arabic translation. But Job was already familiar with the story of Jesus, who is depicted in the Qur'an as a prophet rather than as the incarnation of God in the flesh. Job, like most Muslims, agreed with his Christian sponsors that Jesus was born of the Virgin Mary, performed miracles, and would come again at the end of the world. But he rejected the Christian doctrine of the Trinity, the belief that God, though one in essence, is also three "persons": God the Father, God the Son (Jesus), and God the Holy Spirit.

After he "perused" the Gospels "with a great deal of care," Job told his Christian friends, accurately, that he found no mention of the "Trinity" in the scriptures. Job was quickwitted, using the Christian scriptures to argue for his Islamic theological view of monotheism, the belief in one God. Indeed, though the Gospel of Matthew commands followers of Jesus to baptize the whole world in the name of the "father, son, and holy spirit," the word "trinity" itself is never uttered in the New Testament. Job warned his English hosts to avoid the association of any human images with God, even the image of Prophet Jesus. Job was especially critical—at least according to his Protestant biographer—of Roman Catholic "idolatry," which he had observed in one West African town.

Job's story became the eighteenth-century equivalent of a bestseller. He was a genuine celebrity, earning the patronage of the Duke of Montague. He even met the royal family. The Royal African Company, which hoped that Job might further its trading relationships in West Africa, eventually bought Job's bond and set him free. Then, in 1734, Job returned to his native Africa, arriving safely, "by the will of God," he wrote, at Fort James along the Gambia River. He did not travel to his home region of Bundu immediately, but first accompanied Royal African Company official Francis Moore on a fact-finding mission along the Gambia River. In the meanwhile, a messenger carried correspondence from Job to his family. When the messenger returned, Job received the sad news that his father had died while he was away, and that Bundu had been ravaged by a dreadful war that did not leave even "one cow left."

Despite the threat of thieves and war, in 1735 Job set out with an English colleague for home. When he reached his town, Job fired his guns in the air and galloped his horse wildly in celebration. Job found all his children to be healthy, and he fasted from dawn to dusk for a month, perhaps fulfilling a vow that he had made when he was first captured in 1730 or 1731. Job continued to write to his associates in England, though little is known about his life after 1740. According to one report, he lived a long life and died in 1773 in his native land.

Since 1734, Job's remarkable story has been celebrated, and no doubt embellished, on both sides of the Atlantic. His Arabic letters and the various English-language articles written about him are remarkable documents from the colonial period of North American history. They disprove the notion that Muslims are only recent, foreign additions to North America. Job arrived more than three decades before the United States declared its independence from Great Britain. Though historians still debate exactly how many African Americans in North America were practicing Muslims—estimates range wildly from the thousands to more than a million—there is little doubt that Muslims have been part of the continent's history for hundreds of years. In fact, some Muslims, or Muslims who had converted to Christianity, may have been aboard Columbus's first expedition in 1492.

In the 1530s, the legendary African explorer Estevanico is said to have explored Arizona and New Mexico in search of gold and treasure. A Portuguese slave, Estevanico was also called "the Moor," meaning that he was a Muslim from North

Africa. Whether Estevanico was an actual historical figure remains a matter for debate, though his presence in historical lore reflects, at least symbolically, the likely presence of Muslims among explorers and settlers from the Iberian peninsula. By the late 1500s, common Muslim-sounding names such as Hassan, Osman, Amar, Ali, and Ramadan appeared in Spanish language colonial documents. In the seventeenth and eighteenth centuries, as Job Ben Solomon's biography proves, the question is definitively settled. Various documents by and about American Muslims were published in English and other languages. This evidence establishes that Muslims from almost all Islamic regions of West Africa were present throughout the Americas during the colonial period.

Given Islam's long history and expanding presence in West Africa during the period in which the slave trade took place, some African American slaves were bound to be Muslim. After Islam spread throughout North Africa in the 600s, Berber traders, using camels to cross the Sahara desert, introduced their faith to West African trading partners. In the eighth and ninth centuries, traders and their families peopled various towns in West Africa. By the tenth and eleventh centuries, several West African leaders, including those of Ghana, converted to Islam. This was a pattern repeated often in newly Islamic lands. Islam was at first an elite faith of traders and rulers, but gradually, more and more agrarian people adopted the religion and adapted it to their own life circumstances. From the eleventh to the sixteenth centuries, West African rulers such as Mansa Musa, the fourteenth century king of Mali, built mosques and schools, hired Muslim judges and clerks, and went on pilgrimage to Mecca or gave alms to the poor. Around the time Job Ben Solomon came to North America, Islam was also spreading in Senegal, Gambia, and Guinea, buoyed by family networks of Muslim scholars,

political and military leaders, and mystics who played prominent roles in Muslim West African societies.

Perhaps the most powerful of these elite Muslims captured
in West Africa and brought to the Americas was Abd al-Rahman
Ibrahima, a Muslim noble and military leader from Futa Jalon,
a mountainous region located in what is now Guinea. Like Job
Ben Solomon, Abd al-Rahman was Fulbe, or Fulani, the ethnic group so important to the spread of Islam in West Africa.
In Futa Jalon, the Fulani had succeeded in building a powerful state through military conquest, participation in the slave
trade, and successful cultivation of the fertile region around the
headwaters of the Senegal and Gambia rivers. Like other Fulbe,
Futa Jalon's political and economic leaders also sponsored institutions of Islamic religious life and learning in a capital city,
Timbo, where Abd al-Rahman lived.

Abd al-Rahman claimed to be the son of an *almamy*, a Muslim
noble, and whether the story is completely accurate or not, it is
clear that Abd al-Rahman, who was enslaved while in his twenties,
was a member of the elite class of Futa Jalon. Born around 1762,
Abd al-Rahman benefited from an extensive Islamic education in
Timbuktu and Jenne, two of the great centers of learning in West
Africa. He learned to speak several West African languages, and
like Job Ben Solomon, could also read and write Arabic. After
completing his education, Abd al-Rahman became a warrior, and
he served as a military leader around the same time that that the
ruling Muslim class consolidated its power over the region. On
his way home in 1788 from a successful campaign that extended
the boundaries of his principality to the Atlantic Ocean, Abd al-
Rahman was captured by a rival ethnic group, sent north to the
Gambia River, and sold to European slave traders.

Like many other first-generation Africans who came to the
United States, Abd al-Rahman first landed in the West Indies.

He then was taken to New Orleans, which was a Spanish possession at the time, and finally, hundreds of miles north to Natchez, Mississippi. Using a translator, Abd al-Rahman, like Job Ben Solomon, tried to explain that he was a person of high status in West Africa. His purchaser nicknamed him "Prince," an appellation that he would carry for the rest of his life. Like Job and so many other slaves, Abd al-Rahman hated life in the fields, and he ran away. But after a few weeks wandering in the Mississippi wilderness, he returned to Natchez. Abd al-Rahman married Isabella, an African American Baptist woman, in the 1790s, and as the years passed, they had several children together. He took care of his owner's livestock, kept his own garden, and sold his own produce at the town marketplace. Then, in 1807, as Abd al-Rahman was selling vegetables in Natchez, he was recognized by John Coates Cox, a white man who had stayed in Timbo, and who, it was said, actually knew Abd al-Rahman's father.

Though there is no way to confirm Cox's claims, he maintained that Abd al-Rahman's father had cared for him when he was sick and had provided him with guides so that he might make his way along the Gambia River and eventually return home. Cox, who felt a kinship with Abd al-Rahman, immediately set to work trying to free him. But his appeals to the Mississippi governor and his attempts to purchase Abd al-Rahman's freedom were unsuccessful. Through the use of newspapers, the "prince" did become a local celebrity, though it would be more than two decades before he would achieve national recognition.

Almost two decades later, in 1826, Abd al-Rahman penned a letter in Arabic requesting his freedom. The letter, unusual since it was written in Arabic, was passed along from a U.S. senator to the U.S. consul in Morocco, and finally to Secretary of State Henry Clay. With the support of President John Quincy Adams, Clay personally intervened in the case of Abd al-Rahman, and on behalf of the federal government offered to provide transportation back to Africa for him. But Abd al-Rahman would not leave without freeing his family. Local citizens of Mississippi helped to raise the $200 necessary to free his wife, but Abd al-Rahman would need far greater help and far more generous patrons to raise the thousands of dollars needed to free his eight children. He was single-minded and audacious in achieving that goal.

In April 1828, Abd al-Rahman set out on a nationwide tour in order to raise the money he needed. With Secretary of State Henry Clay's endorsement, important merchants, politicians, and philanthropists opened their homes, their assembly halls, and their pocketbooks to him. As he traveled along the eastern seaboard of the United States, he met Francis Scott Key, the author of "The Star-Spangled Banner"; Charles and Arthur Tappan, wealthy Christian reformers who later funded the movement to abolish slavery; Edward Everett, a Massachusetts representative in the U.S. Congress; and Thomas Gallaudet, the founder of America's first important school for the deaf. He was also feted by prominent African American civic groups such as the Black Masons of Boston, whose second marshal, David Walker, would soon write his manifesto of black liberation called the *Appeal to the Colored Citizens of the World* (1829).

When speaking with merchants, Abd al-Rahman promised to further their economic interests; when conversing with members of the American Colonization Society, which wanted to send African Americans "back to Africa," he endorsed their plans; and when meeting with missionaries, he pledged to spread Christianity in West Africa. He played the "Arab prince" when necessary, donning a Moorish costume to mark himself as exotic and different from other African Americans. This attempt to use an "Oriental" identity to his own advantage was based on the sound assumption that many whites would see him, as Henry Clay did, not as a black African but as a member of the Moorish "race," a tragic Muslim prince who had been the "unfortunate" victim of fate.

These were all temporary strategies fabricated by Abd al-Rahman to achieve a larger and more personal objective. When some of his hosts asked him to write the Lord's Prayer in Arabic, he indeed wrote something in Arabic, but it was the *Fatiha*, the opening chapter of the Qur'an used by Muslims as part of their daily prayers and other devotions. Abd al-Rahman was also a willing critic of white American Christian hypocrisy. While unpopular among some of his patrons, these sentiments would have been welcomed by his abolitionist benefactors, who believed that slavery was a stain on the soul of America.

Like Job Ben Solomon, Abd al-Rahman was familiar with both Christian theology and scriptures, and according to reporter Cyrus Griffin of the *Natchez Southern Galaxy*, once said that the New "Testament [was] very good law; [but] you no follow it." He criticized the lack of piety that he observed: "You no pray often enough." He claimed that Christians used their religion to justify their greed and cruel use of slaves: "You greedy after money. You good man, you join the religion? See, you want more land, more niggers; you make nigger work hard, make more cotton. Where you find that in your law?" Many prominent abolitionists up north could not have said it better themselves. Abd al-Rahman knew what his audiences wanted to hear, and as a result, his ten-month fundraising tour met its goal, collecting the incredible sum (for that time) of $3,400.

In February 1829, sixty-something-year-old Abd al-Rahman and his wife, Isabella, departed from the port at Norfolk, Virginia, on the *Harriet* for Liberia, the African American colony in West Africa. More than four decades had passed since he had been forced to leave his native land. Abd al-Rahman's plan was to wait for the rainy season to finish, and then to make the journey from Liberia to Timbo. But after arriving safely in Monrovia, the country's capital, he fell ill with fever and diarrhea, and in early July 1829, Abd al-Rahman died.

In 1830, the committee of supporters who had helped Abd al-Rahman stage his fundraising tour fulfilled his promise by purchasing the freedom of at least four of his sons. In the summer of that year, the committee arranged for the transport of two of them, Simon and Levi, to Africa. They arrived in Monrovia that December, where they rejoined their mother, the American-born Baptist wife of a West African Muslim noble. Sons Prince and Abraham, though freed, stayed in the United States, while at least three of his children remained enslaved. Generation and after generation of Abd al-Rahman's descendants—hundreds, if not thousands of Americans—came to trace their lineage to this important, if under-explored figure of U.S. history.

Both Job Ben Solomon and Abd al-Rahman were literate and urbane Muslims who used their knowledge, talents, and, when necessary, legerdemain, to improve their daily living conditions under slavery and to return home to Africa. To achieve such goals, they had to rely on the interests of various white people. In both cases, some merchants and venture capitalists were anxious to know more about the lands from which Job and Abd al-Rahman had come so that they might better exploit the natural and human resources of those regions.

American slaveholders wanted to understand the ethnic identities of slaves such as Job and Abd al-Rahman so that they might better use and control them; for them, these Muslims were quite literally a breed apart. Christian missionaries also used the stories of these Muslims to raise funds for their efforts to win souls for Christ rather than Allah and to show that

Africans were capable of benefiting from schooling and other institutions of "civilization." In the case of Abd al-Rahman, abolitionists seized upon the image of the noble African to show the inherent humanity and intelligence of slaves.

Navigating these white interests would become even more complicated for African American Muslims—and African Americans more generally—after 1831, when Nat Turner's relatively successful slave revolt in Virginia crystallized the fear among whites that they were sitting on a powder keg of slave dissent. Constitutional rights of free expression, freedom of religion, and freedom of assembly were severely curtailed for all southerners, especially African Americans. Though some historians have emphasized this period of antebellum southern history as one in which slaves subtly negotiated the terms of their enslavement, others see this period as akin to a state of war in which slaveholders, and those aligned with them, employed any degree of violence and repression to maintain their privileged position in U.S. society. African American Muslim slaves, like slaves more generally, used whatever means were at their disposal to improve their lives and to gain their freedom.

For Omar ibn Sayyid, that meant publicly converting to Christianity, or perhaps pretending to convert to Christianity, and writing poetry praising his master. Omar ibn Sayyid, like both Job and Abd al-Rahman, was an ethnic Fulbe or Fulani from West Africa. Born in Futa Toro, he was from the northern region of modern Senegal, where Islam was flourishing in the era of his youth. For more than two decades, Omar studied the Qur'an; the *hadith*, or the sayings and deeds of the Prophet Muhammad and his companions; and the Islamic religious sciences. He may have been a trader, a warrior, a teacher—or all three—before he was captured and sold into slavery. He arrived in Charleston, South Carolina, around 1807. One of his early owners was so cruel, he said, that he escaped to Fayetteville, North Carolina. But Omar was caught and jailed, then sold again. This time, Omar convinced his new owner, Jim Owen, that he was, in his own words, "a man of weak eyes" and "weak body," an intellectual, and a spiritually inclined person who was not capable of or suited for hard labor.

Omar never returned to Africa. He attended a local church and remained a bachelor the rest of his days. Like Abd al-Rahman, he was celebrated by journalists and writers as an Arabian prince who had come to embrace Christianity. Omar also wrote letters, and like Abd al-Rahman, was asked by various white Christians to render the Lord's Prayer and other Christian scriptures in Arabic. Such performances may have left otherwise unwitting audiences with the impression that Omar had indeed converted to Christianity, although the substance of his writing gives a much more ambiguous portrait of Omar's religious convictions. During the perilous years in which he was composing such documents, it would have been dangerous for Omar to write, even in Arabic, that Christianity was a religious distortion, and that he remained a Muslim in his heart.

In 1819, a local leader of the American Colonization Society (ACS), North Carolina judge John Louis Taylor sent one of Omar's earliest known letters to Francis Scott Key, a founder of the ACS, which hoped to repatriate black slaves to Africa. Taylor was dismayed that Omar was Muslim and requested an Arabic Bible so that he might convince him to convert to Christianity. Omar's letter indicated that such a conversion was unlikely. Citing both the Qur'an and the *hadith*, Omar complained that "what you have been told by your fathers is not true. You show God in male or female form? Behold, such is an unfair division!" In other words, Omar was criticizing the Christian belief in the Incarnation, the idea that God appeared in the human flesh of Jesus, and the belief that God could be "divided" into different forms. For Omar, God was One. "These are nothing but names which you have made up—you and your fathers," he concluded (Qur'an 53:21–23).

Certainly Omar believed in Jesus, but only as a prophet, as he suggested by quoting Qur'an 2:285, in which people of faith declare that they make no distinctions between all of the apostles of God. All apostles are worthy of respect and tellers of truth, Omar seemed to be arguing, but no apostle is a god. In the letter's conclusion, Omar's thoughts drifted to the Day of Judgment as he remembered the Qur'anic teaching that God places on no soul a greater burden than it can bear (2:286). He asked God's forgiveness in the land of unbelievers, and he pleaded that when the world comes to an end, he would be transported back to Africa for final judgment.

Although no later document from Omar's hand presents similar criticisms of Christianity, his later writings make one question whether Omar ever really converted to Christianity. Omar's autobiography, written in 1831, is the only known Arabic-language autobiography written by a North American slave. It is a document full of dissimulation, the hiding of one's true religious identity. Omar began his autobiography by invoking the name of God, the merciful, the compassionate, and asking blessings on the Prophet Muhammad. He also quoted extensively from one of the most popular chapters of the Qur'an, called Sura al-Mulk, "the chapter of Dominion," or God's sovereignty. This *sura*, or chapter of the Qur'an, asks its readers to ponder God's power over every aspect of creation, to remember that God created life and death, and to mourn human beings who have lost sight of God. In the historical context in which Omar was writing, it would not be unreasonable to interpret such statements as antislavery sentiments—the concept that dominion belongs completely to God, not to other men.

As Omar's autobiography continued, he recounted his enslavement, his mistreatment at the hands of a terrible owner, and his utter relief at being sold to Jim Owen. "O ye people of North Carolina," he wrote, "O ye people of South Carolina, O ye people of America all of you, have you among you any...such men as Jim Owen?" Omar also juxtaposed his American trials with life back home. Before he came to a Christian country, he professed, "I walked to the mosque before day-break, washed my face and head and hands and feet. I prayed at noon, prayed in the afternoon, prayed at sunset, prayed in the evening. I gave alms every year....I went on pilgrimage to Mecca." Such comments reveal how much these Islamic traditions had informed his identity in Africa. But the Owens family read the Gospel to him, he said, and though he once prayed in the words of the *Fatiha*, the first chapter of the Qur'an, he now prayed in the words of the Lord's Prayer. The autobiography ended not with lofty religious sentiments, but with more words of praise for the relative kindness of his owner, Jim Owen.

The ambiguity of Omar's autobiography reminds us how all writing is shaped by the time and place in which it is composed. His autobiography is short on the details of what it was like to practice Islamic religion in North America. Because so much of slave religion in North America—whether Islamic, Christian, or African traditional religion—was clandestine in nature, it is possible that much Muslim religious activity went on without notice. Even when whites observed African American Muslim rituals, they often did not understand what was taking place right in front of their eyes. Notwithstanding this fact, there is no evidence to suggest that Omar practiced Islam in a communal setting with other Muslim slaves. In fact, by all accounts he was largely a solitary human being. Whether the historical accounts of Omar—as well as Job and Abd al-Rahman—omit critical details about the presence of a practicing community of Muslim slaves in North America, we will likely never know. To find evidence that Islam was practiced in a communal setting, we must look to other sources.

Around the Georgia and South Carolina coasts, African American Muslim slaves and free men and women of color practiced Islam in the nineteenth century and perhaps into the early twentieth century as well. These Muslims lived in relatively isolated communities such as St. Simons Island and Sapelo Island, Georgia, where plantations were generally large and blacks often outnumbered whites as a percentage of the area's total population. African traditions, including Islam, were more likely to survive the middle passage if a community of people was committed to their perpetuation. On Sapelo Island, a Muslim slave named Bilali, also called Ben Ali, Belali Mahomet, and Bu Allah, became a successful overseer and father of a large family. Bilali's master, Thomas Spaulding, owned thousands of acres on Sapelo Island, where African Americans lived together in villages and raised cotton, sugar cane, and rice. There were very few whites on the island, and Spaulding put Bilali in charge of hundreds of slaves. Bilali was credited with successfully preparing these slaves to fight off the British in the War of 1812 and evacuating them to safety during the hurricane of 1824.

First brought to the Bahamas from Futa Jalon in Guinea—also the homeland of Abd al-Rahman—Bilali married and had children in the islands. He married again and had more children after his arrival in Georgia. Though some of Bilali's biographers have used this evidence to label Bilali a Muslim polygamist, the fact that Bilali may have had more than one wife was not unusual in slave communities. Slaves were chattel, and owners constantly broke apart slave families by selling husbands, wives, and children to different owners in different places. The result was that African American male and female slaves often remarried, whether formally or informally. Even more, African American slaves developed a communal consciousness that went beyond blood, as they cared for orphaned children and others who had been torn from their homes and forced to move elsewhere.

Because of his relative privilege as an overseer, however, Bilali was able to keep his family together and raised all twelve sons and seven daughters on Sapelo. One white woman from Broughton Island, Georgia, met Bilali's children in the late 1850s and recorded her impressions that they were "tall and well-formed" and spoke a language—probably Fula—that she did not understand. She also noted that the family "worshipped Mahomet," or Muhammad. That detail is important since it suggests that Bilali, like some other Muslim coastal residents, may have been able to pass on elements of his religious culture to his children.

Bilali was literate and educated, and like other Muslims slaves, left behind physical evidence of his learning. One of his Arabic manuscripts, now preserved at the University of Georgia, contains selections from a legal treatise popular in West Africa among followers of the Maliki school of *shari'a*, or Islamic law and ethics. Like Omar ibn Sayyid and others, Bilali probably began his education by memorizing the Qur'an and some of the Sunna, or traditions of the Prophet Muhammad. Perhaps Bilali also had exposure to Islamic higher education, which generally included the study of qur'anic commentary, theology, and grammar. Even so, several errors mar Bilali's manuscript, indicating that when he wrote it, he may have forgotten parts of the manuscript or left school before his education was complete. There is no evidence to suggest that he passed on Arabic literacy and Islamic higher education to his children. But according to Bilali's descendants and those who knew them in Georgia, he did encourage in them a sense of their Muslim identity and knowledge of Islamic religious practice.

Bilali's descendants shared this information with workers from the Savannah unit of the Georgia Writers Project, a federally funded program of President Franklin D. Roosevelt's Works Projects Administration (WPA). In Georgia and around the country, field workers were employed in the 1930s to record the oral histories of people whose ethnic traditions were being lost or transformed in modern America. Because of these records, we can paint a rich picture of religious life among African American Muslims from the Georgia coast. Some of the most noteworthy oral histories, unlike the written biographies from the eighteenth and nineteenth centuries, describe the religious lives of African American Muslim women.

For example, Sapelo Island resident Katie Brown was the great-granddaughter of Bilali. She remembered the names of Bilali's daughters, some of whom had Anglo names like Margaret and others who were called Medina and Fatima, which were African and Muslim names. Brown said that her grandmother and another relative told her that Bilali and his wife Phoebe "was very particular about the time they pray and they was very regular about the hour; [they prayed] when the sun come up, when it straight over the head, and when it set." Praying three times a day was a standard religious practice in many Islamic traditions, including some of those in West Africa. Three times a day Bilali and Phoebe would prostrate themselves on a prayer rug and "bow to the sun," that is to the east—toward Mecca.

In addition, she reported that "Bilali and his wife Phoebe prayed on the bead," meaning that they used Muslim prayer beads to perform *dhikr*, a meditative form of prayer in which the believer remembers the presence of God by repeating the names of God or short sayings. Shad Hall, another of Bilali's descendants, also remembered his grandmother Hester and several family members using beads when they prayed. Bilali, said Katie Brown, would pull each bead on the long string, and recite words of devotion to God and his prophet, Muhammad. The fact that Bilali used a long string of beads may indicate that he owned the same kind of beads popular among the Qadiriyya, a Sufi order, or pietistic group that had a profound impact on West African politics and society in this era.

The Muslims of the coastal region also preserved some African holidays, especially the annual celebration of *sadaka* or *saraka*. During this festival, which was often celebrated in West Africa to commemorate ancestors, to offer thanks, or to ask for help, Katie Brown remembered that her grandmother would make "funny flat cake she call 'saraka.'" The recipe, a variation on West African cooking, involved soaking rice in water overnight, and then pounding the swollen, softened rice in a wooden mortar with a pestle until it turned into paste. Then Brown's grandmother would add honey and sometimes sugar, and form the paste into flat cakes. "She make them same day every year," recalled Brown, "and it a big day. When they finish, she call us in, all the children, and put in hands little flat cake. And we eats it." Shad Hall's grandmother, Hester, would offer a blessing on the cakes by saying, "Ameen, Ameen, Ameen" (the Arabic word for Amen) before eating them.

Brown also recalled that her grandmother, Margaret, wore some type of *hijab*, or head scarf. Margaret, who was born in the Bahamas, donned "a loose white cloth that she throw over her head like veil and it hang loose on her shoulder. I ain't know why she wear it that way," her granddaughter remarked, "but I think she ain't like a tight thing round her head." Whether this head scarf had a specifically Islamic meaning for Katie Brown's grandmother is not clear. Sometimes a head scarf is just a head scarf. In addition, its meaning may have changed over the years in Sapelo Island.

One of the difficulties more generally in reconstructing religious life among African American slaves is figuring out when and where African Americans transformed certain African practices to suit their new environment or to meet new social needs. At times, it is clear that slaves combined the old with the new. According to the Rev. Charles Colcock Jones, a Georgia farmer and preacher, some slaves who became Christians in the South were not dissimulating; they claimed that Christianity and Islam were two expression of the same religious idea: "God, they say, is Allah, and Jesus Christ is Mohammed—the religion is the same, but different countries have different names."

On the Georgia coast, however, Muslim religious practice before the Civil War was far more likely to be performed alongside African traditional religion rather than alongside Christianity, which may not have become the majority religion among African Americans on the island until the Reconstruction and Jim Crow eras of U.S. history. Nero Jones, like others interviewed by WPA workers, remembered that when local residents celebrated the harvest festival, they would spend the night singing and praying. Then, after the sun came up, they would dance, beat their drums, and shake rattles made out of dried gourds. Participants in this dance, which was called the ring shout, moved in a counterclockwise direction and fell into a trance. The fact that Nero Jones's family members performed the shout did not preclude their performance of Muslim rituals as well, and perhaps they did not see any contradiction between African traditional religion and Islam. Jones recalled that his aunt and uncle were "mighty particular about praying." Like Bilali and Phoebe, they used prayer beads and recited Arabic words with which Jones was unfamiliar.

Some African American Muslims on the coast practiced a form of Islam that combined Islamic rituals with elements of hoodoo or conjure, the African American folk religious practice of healing and harming that involves the use of material objects—the religious activity labeled pejoratively as magic and superstition. Rosa Grant described childhood memories of her grandmother, Ryna, a first-generation African American, praying in the morning: "Every morning at sun-up, she kneel on the floor in a room and bow over and touch her head to the floor three time. Then she say a prayer. I don't remember what just what she say, but one word she say used to make us children laugh. I remember it was 'ashamnegad.' When she finish praying, she say, 'Ameen, ameen, ameen.'" Grant also remembered that her grandmother called Friday "her prayer day," probably referring to the Islamic tradition of congregational prayers on that day. These recollections establish that Rosa's grandmother was a practicing Muslim.

At the same time, this Muslim woman engaged in hoodoo. "She talk plenty about conjure," said Grant. "She say that when a person been made to swell up from an evil spell, they got to have somebody to pray and drag for them. If you have a pain or a misery in the leg or arm, you kill a black chicken and split it open and slap it where the pain is, and that will cure the pain."

Some Muslims in the area seemed to frown on such practices as superstitious. According to James Hamilton Couper, the owner of Salih Bilali on St. Simon Island, Salih Bilali was a strict Muslim who "abstains from spirituous liquors, and keeps the various fasts," including the dawn-to-sunset fast conducted every day during the Islamic month of Ramadan. The Muslim was "singularly exempt from all superstition; and holds in great contempt the African belief in fetishes and evil spirits." Couper never explained exactly what separated legitimate religion from illegitimate superstition for Salih Bilali, but we can guess that he might have opposed killing a chicken to heal an illness. Instead, he or others like him might have suggested that a patient place an amulet containing passages of the Qur'an around his neck or recite certain litanies using his prayer beads. Such practices virtually defined Muslim piety in West Africa during this time.

For African American Muslims and African American slaves more generally, however, Salih Bilali's criticism of African traditional religion as magic and superstition was probably a minority point of view. Slaves often used any religious practice that they believed would lift the human spirit above the dehumanizing conditions under which they were forced to live. Rosa Grant's grandmother, Ryna, was one such slave. Captured in Africa, Ryna was a little girl when she was forced into slavery with her mother, Theresa. After "they been here a while," said Rosa Grant, "the mother get to where she can't stand it and she want to go back to Africa. One day my gran, Ryna, was standing with her [mother] in the field." Theresa swirled her body around twice, said Rosa. "She stretch her arms out." Then, she "rise right up and fly back to Africa."

Ryna was not the only slave who testified to this miraculous journey back to Africa. Another Georgia woman remembered similar stories. This interviewee said that her grandmother, Rachel Grant, was a Muslim who prayed three times a day. "She always face the sun," remembered her granddaughter, "and when she finish praying she always bow to the sun. She tell me about the slaves what could fly too. If they didn't like it on the plantation, they just take wing and fly right back to Africa."

Perhaps for Muslim slaves such as Rachel Grant there was a connection between prayer and the slaves "what could fly." If your body could not be transported back home, then at least your spirit could. You faced east, in the direction of both Mecca and your home, and you prayed to the God who had ultimate sovereignty, over all affairs both human and divine. As you bowed at the waist and touched your head to the earth, your spirit took flight to Africa and was restored. Whether or not that was the experience of African American Muslim slaves, many African American Muslims in the twentieth century would testify later that by practicing Islam, they were reclaiming a religious and spiritual heritage that had been stolen from them when their ancestors were kidnapped in Africa. Their desire to reconnect with a Muslim past, like those slaves who faced east, pointed not only toward Africa but also toward Mecca, the axis of the worldwide Muslim community. The religious imaginations of twentieth-century African American Muslims leapt across the Atlantic and so did their bodies, as they visited West Africa and Egypt, made pilgrimage to Mecca in Arabia, and toured Pakistan and other Muslim-majority countries. For many of them, such travel felt like a homecoming.

In 1831, Omar ibn Sayyid, a North Carolina slave who may or may not have converted to Christianity, penned a short memoir in Arabic. In addition to recounting the details of his life in the United States, the manuscript contained a prologue excerpting a long passage from the qur'anic chapter entitled al-Mulk, *or Power. This chapter of the Qur'an juxtaposes God's dominion over all things with the feeble attempts of human beings to control their own destinies. By including this passage, perhaps Omar ibn Sayyid was reminding himself that he was not master of the fate that had befallen him, and that while an earthly master claimed to own him, he truly belonged to God.*

In the name of God, the merciful the gracious. God grant his blessing upon our Prophet Mohammed. Blessed be He in whose hands is the kingdom and who is Almighty; who created death and life that he might test You; for he is exalted; he is the forgiver (of sins), who created seven heavens one above the other....

I cannot write my life because I have forgotten much of my own language, as well as of the Arabic. Do not be hard upon me, my brother. To God let many thanks be paid for his great mercy and goodness.

My name is Omar ibn Seid [Said or Sayyid]. My birthplace was Fut Tur, between the two rivers. I sought knowledge under the instruction of a Sheikh called Mohammed Seid, my own brother, and Sheikh Soleiman Kembeh, and Sheikh Gabriel Abdal. I continued my studies twenty-five years, and then returned to my home where I remained six years. Then there came to our place a large army, who killed many men, and took me, and brought me to the great sea, and sold me into the hands of the Christians, who bound me and sent me on board a great ship and we sailed upon the great sea a month and a half, when we came to a place called Charleston in the Christian language. There they sold me to a small, weak, and wicked man called Johnson, a complete infidel, who had no fear of God at all. Now I am a small man, and unable to do hard work so I fled from the hand of Johnson and after a month came to a place called Fayd-il [Fayetteville, N.C.].

There I saw some great houses (churches). On the new moon I went into a church to pray. A lad saw me and rode off to the place of his father and informed him that he had seen a black man in the church. A man named Handah (Hunter?) and another man with him on horseback came attended by a troop of dogs. They took me and made me go with them twelve miles to a place called Fayd-il, where they put me into a great house from which I could not go out. I continued in the great house (which, in the Christian language, they called *jail*) sixteen days and nights. One Friday the jailor came and opened the door of the house and I saw a great many men, all Christians, some of whom called out to me, "What is your name? Is it Omar or Seid?" I did not understand their Christian language. A man called Bob Mumford took me and led me out of the jail, and I was very well pleased to go with them to their place. I stayed at Mumford's four days and nights, and then a man named Jim Owen, son-in-law of Mumford, having married his daughter Betsey, asked me if I was willing to go to a place called Bladen. I said, Yes, I was willing. I went with them and have remained in the place of Jim Owen until now.

CHAPTER TWO

The First American Converts to Islam

A t first glance, he was an unlikely candidate for conversion to Islam. Born in 1846, Alexander Russell Webb hailed from a white, Protestant, middle-class family of printers and newspapermen in Hudson, New York. As a child, he attended Hudson-on-the-Hudson's First Presbyterian Church, whose members included some of the town's most powerful citizens— men such as U.S. President Martin van Buren. Despite or perhaps because of his relative position of social privilege, Webb became a religious rebel at a young age. He did not believe in the doctrine of the Trinity and he found listening to his preacher's sermons far less spiritual than playing outdoors in God's green earth. After the Civil War, as a young man in his twenties, Webb moved to Chicago and began a jewelry business. In 1871, this venture, like so many others, was lost during the great Chicago fire. Around the same time, Webb also formally abandoned his Christian faith and eschewed all forms of religious belief. He relied, for a time, only on reason and science for answers to his questions about the meaning of life.

In 1874, Webb moved to Missouri, where he started life over as a journalist. In the next several years, he worked for the *Unionville Republican*, the *St. Joseph Gazette*, the *St. Louis Post-Dispatch*, the *St. Louis Globe-Democrat*, and the *Missouri Republican*. During this period of Webb's life, the newspaperman turned away from his flirtations with atheism toward alternative forms of religion and spirituality. Like some other religious seekers in an era of U.S. history that Mark Twain dubbed the Gilded Age, Webb first explored spiritualism, a religious tradition that emphasizes communing with the dead as a way to bridge the gap between the material world and the world of the spirits. Webb also became attracted to theosophy, the religious movement established in the 1870s and 1880s by Madame Helena Blavatsky, a Russian spiritualist, and Henry Steel Olcott, an American army officer. Theosophists were devoted to studying the spiritual and inner wisdom of all world religions, but especially emphasized the sagacity of "Oriental" religions such as Buddhism and Hinduism.

Like other intellectually minded theosophists, Webb devoted hours a day to studying books about the mystic East and its spiritual secrets. Especially interested in the mystical aspects of Islam, in 1886 or 1887 he also launched an international series of written exchanges with Ghulam Ahmad, a Muslim reformer in India. Ahmad was a self-proclaimed modern Muslim who sought to counter the gains made by colonial Christian missionaries in South Asia. In writing to Ahmad, Webb wanted to make sure that Ahmad was not an Islamic partisan. "You recognize the truths that underlie all religions," Webb tried to confirm in a letter to Ahmad, "and not their exoteric features which have been added by men." For Webb, all religions were one in spirit even if their ritual and outer elements differed.

Webb's correspondence with Ahmad signaled his desire to engage with Muslims from overseas. To truly imbibe the religion's inner truths, Webb figured, he would have to travel to Muslim lands and study with real Muslims on their turf. That opportunity seemingly appeared in 1887, when his political connections as a Democratic newspaperman yielded him an appointment by President Grover Cleveland as U.S. consul to the Philippines, a chain of islands "in the East" then under Spanish colonial control. On November 9, Webb and his family left San Francisco for the Filipino capital city of Manila, where Webb thought he might be able to meet and study with Muslims. As it turned out, Webb did not meet indigenous Filipino Muslims, many of whom lived in Mindanao, an island far from Manila. But he was able to make contact with Muslim visitors to the Philippines, and his relatively light duties as a diplomat, if maddeningly bureaucratic, allowed Webb adequate time to continue his intellectual study of Islam.

Sometime after arriving in Manila, Webb formally declared himself a convert to Islam. He also struck up a correspondence with another Muslim from India, a Bombay merchant named Budruddin Kur. Soon, Webb began publishing English articles about Islam in India's *Allahabad Review*. These writings advocated the establishment of an Islamic mission in America and encouraged Muslims in India to support the endeavor. Kur apparently concurred and shared news of this white American convert with Hajee Abdulla Arab, a successful Calcutta businessman. Arab became interested in funding Webb's mission. In 1892, Arab visited Webb in Manila to negotiate the details. That same year, Webb resigned his post as U.S. Consul and set off on an Indian fundraising tour that was arranged by his new Muslim brothers.

Traveling first by sea to Singapore, Burma, and Calcutta, then by rail to Bombay, Hyderabad, Madras, and Agra, among other South Asian cities, Webb met with powerful Muslim land-holders, foreign Muslim visitors and diplomats, Muslim merchants, and Muslim holy men, many of whom blessed him and his desire to establish an American Islamic mission. With pledges of financial and moral support, Webb left India for New York, where in 1893, he officially established the "American Islamic Propaganda," wrote the book *Islam in America*, started a periodical called *The Moslem World*, and set up a Manhattan office as the headquarters for his mission. Webb's missionary efforts attracted the attention of the press, and he was even selected as the Muslim representative to the Parliament of Religions at the Chicago World's Fair of 1893. In all these venues, Webb promoted Islam as a religion that expressed some of America's most deeply held values, especially those of rationality, human equality, broadmindedness, and an acceptance of religious diversity.

Despite Webb's initial splash on the national scene, however, he was unable to sustain his mission for more than three years. Few Americans actually converted to Islam under his tutelage. It was true that a great many other liberally minded Americans, especially theosophists, expressed sympathy for Webb's propagation of the "mystical knowledge of the East" in America. But these people did not offer Webb the kind of financial support necessary to carry on his high-profile work. Much of the money promised by his Indian patrons never materialized. Subscriptions to his periodical did not produce enough income to fill the gap. To be sure, Webb had very little time to build his mission and his constituency, but his lack of success in attracting converts and financial support was also a result of his decision to gear his message exclusively toward "respectable," white, well-educated, and "thinking" middle-class Americans.

When he began his mission in 1893, Webb told the *New York Times* that he wanted nothing to do with the Muslim peddlers and other working-class Muslim immigrants from the Middle East and South Asia who already lived in New York.

That Webb could even consider targeting white, middle-class Americans for conversion reflected a change in American attitudes toward Islam and Muslims during the nineteenth century. Though the Muslim world was still seen as violent, fanatical, sexist, and dangerous by many Americans in Webb's era, it was also increasingly understood as romantic, adventurous, and, for religious liberals like Webb, innately spiritual. On the pages of his publications, Webb promoted Islamic religion as a spiritual resource in the battle against what he and other religious seekers viewed as an overly materialistic and spiritually moribund American culture. But the fact that many cartoonists and journalists of the era lampooned Webb and his conversion indicates that many Americans were not ready to divorce themselves from their more exotic ideas about Islam and the Muslim lands. Many Americans were simply unable to see Islam in the way that Webb had framed it.

Though Webb's organization and his publications largely disappeared from public view, his view of Islam as liberal, spiritual, and modern remained a part of America's religious scene in the early twentieth century. As Webb himself faded from national prominence, another Muslim missionary would attract newspaper headlines and the attention of some of America's most prominent religious liberals. In 1910, the Indian musician and religious leader Inayat Khan traveled throughout the United States, where he was received most warmly in New York, Los Angeles, and San Francisco. Khan was a Sufi or mystically minded Muslim, meaning that he actively cultivated an intimate and spiritual relationship to God through prayer, meditation, and other rituals meant to bring the believer closer to the Divine.

Khan, like Webb, taught that the essential message of Islam was its unity with all other great religions, and that all believers in truth should cooperate and even worship with one another, no matter what their particular religious affiliation. In marrying a U.S. citizen, Ora Ray Baker, a relative of Christian Science founder Mary Baker Eddy, he showed just how committed he was to the possibility of a cross-cultural, inter-religious community. During his stay in the United States, from 1910 to 1912, he convinced at least a few others that they should devote their lives to what he called "spiritual contemplation and the service of humanity."

But the Sufi master was disappointed by most of his American audiences. Most people came merely to be amused, not to seek metaphysical truth. They were looking to be entertained, not spiritually challenged. Khan noted that Sufi teachings were treated as a fashion that could be discarded as soon as the next fad appeared in the American religious marketplace. "For the Message," he wrote later, "the time was not yet ripe." Khan admired American devotion to progress and modernity, but he was critical of American racism, the unfettered love of material goods, and the incredible pace of American life. He moved on to Europe, but the impact of his work as one of the first Muslim missionaries in the United States lives on into the present. One of the oldest, continuing operating Sufi organizations in the United States, the Sufi Order of the West, now Sufi Order International, was led first by his son, Vilayat Khan, and then by his grandson, Zia Khan. And other Sufi groups, including the International Sufi movement and Sufi Ruhaniat International, have also been devoted to his teachings.

Khan was not the only Muslim missionary from South Asia to seek Muslim converts during the first two decades of the twentieth century. In fact, Indian missionary Mufti Muhammad Sadiq would have an even larger impact than Khan on the spread of Islam in the United States. A follower of Ghulam Ahmad, the Indian reformer with whom Webb had corresponded decades before, Sadiq arrived in New York in 1920. He was a missionary for the movement that had been formed around the teachings of Ahmad, a group called the Ahmadiyya. Ahmadi Muslims, like Inayat Khan's Sufi Muslims, advocated a peaceful, open-minded, and spiritual interpretation of Islam, but also emphasized the teachings of their founder, Ghulam Ahmad.

Ahmadi Muslims believed that Ghulam Ahmad was the long-promised Christian Messiah and the Islamic Mahdi, a figure in Islamic tradition who will bring peace and justice to the world before the Day of Judgment. Many also thought that Ghulam Ahmad was a prophet. These claims about Ahmad separated the Ahmadiyya from most other Muslims, who condemned them as heretics for declaring that there was a prophet after Muhammad. For most Muslims, Muhammad of Arabia was the "seal of the prophets" and the final messenger of God to humanity. In 1920, however, most Americans knew little about such internal disputes within the world of Islamic religion. For most who met the Ahmadi missionary, Sadiq was just another exotic Easterner who practiced the "Oriental" religion of Islam.

Unlike previous missionaries, Muhammad Sadiq quickly adjusted his missionary techniques and goals to meet the demands of sustaining a successful mission in America. Establishing a permanent mission on Chicago's South Side, Sadiq soon realized that African Americans were far more receptive to his message than whites. Many of these African Americans had come to the urban North from their predominantly rural homes in the South as part of the Great Migration, which occurred during the first half of the twentieth century. Some of them joined existing churches, especially the black Baptist and black Methodist congregations. Others created their own religious organizations. Faced with new economic challenges, exposed to new people and ideas, and seeking new social networks, these migrants contributed to the growth of Pentecostal and Holiness churches, Catholic churches, Father Divine's Peace Mission movement, and Bishop Daddy Grace's Universal House of Prayer for All People.

The Ahmadiyya also benefited from the presence of these migrants, and it tailored a religious message that was attractive to them and to other African Americans. Missionary Muhammad Sadiq emphasized his belief that Islam was a universal religion for all people and strongly advocated social equality for African Americans. The Ahmadiyya newspaper, the *Moslem Sunrise*, regularly featured articles critical of Christian racism—an easy claim to prove in the 1920s, as the Ku Klux Klan rose to political and social prominence based partly on its appeal to a white Protestant version of Christianity. This white brand of Christianity, one *Moslem Sunrise* article proclaimed, had supported slavery and had destroyed black people's connections to their true religious heritage, which was Islam, and to their original language, which was Arabic. "You need a religion," the article declared, "which teaches manliness, self-reliance, self-respect, and self-effort."

The Ahmadiyya movement also supported the Universal Negro Improvement Association (UNIA), a mass movement founded by the Jamaican leader Marcus Garvey that sought to encourage racial unity among all people of African descent, spawn the growth of black-owned businesses, and establish an independent nation in Africa. Ahmadi leaders in the United States hoped that the Garvey movement would choose Islam as the official religion of the movement, arguing that Islam "would be a wonderful spiritual force in the life of the colored races, uniting us in a bond of common sympathy and interest." As a missionary movement born partly to counter the influence of missionary Christianity's spread in British India, the Ahmadiyya contended that people of Asian and African descent shared a common bond as the victims of European imperial aggression. Ahmadi missionary Muhammad Sadiq took that message to various meetings of the UNIA and reportedly converted dozens of UNIA members to Islam.

Ahmadi missionaries had discovered a growing trend among English-speaking black people in the Americas, Great Britain, and Africa: some of them increasingly identified the Islamic religion as a source of racial pride, educational achievement, cultural refinement, and political self-determination. It had begun perhaps with the educator and politician Edward Wilmot Blyden, an African American from the Caribbean who had moved to the West African nation of Liberia in 1851. After traveling extensively among African "natives" in the West African interior, Blyden concluded that Islam, as opposed to Christianity, had succeeded in producing genuine black civilization, self-respect, high morals, industry, deep spirituality, and social unity. His writings, collected in the 1887 book *Christianity, Islam, and the Negro Race*, continued to be read long after Blyden died in 1912, and many of his ideas became common knowledge in the Garvey movement and other organizations committed to the political self-determination of black people—most of whom still could not vote in 1920s America.

But African Americans were attracted to Islam in that decade not only for political reasons but for religious reasons as well. In St. Louis, Missouri, for example, P. Nathaniel Johnson, an African American who changed his name to Ahmad Din, became the leader of a multiracial Ahmadi mosque that included blacks, whites, and Muslim immigrants. In explaining why he became a Muslim, Ahmad Din wrote in the *Moslem Sunrise* that after surveying the sacred texts of the world, he found the Qur'an to be the best. The mere fact that Ahmad Din could obtain an English translation of the Qur'an was another reason for the Ahmadiyya's early success—for they were the first group to mass distribute translations of the Qur'an as part of an American missionary effort. The Qur'an, Ahmad Din wrote, was "a poem, a code of laws, a prayer book, and the world's best bible combined." Other scriptures were an "aggregation of poets, prophets, prophetesses, statesmen, and lawgivers, historically covering thousand of years, crammed full of conflicting statements." But the Qur'an, he declared, was different. It came exclusively from the mouth of Muhammad. Ahmad Din compared Muhammad to a "master spiritualist," one who was "intoxicated with the gifts of God."

While hundreds, probably thousands of African American men and women followed in Ahmad Din's footsteps by joining the Ahmadiyya movement, other African American Muslims formed their own indigenous Muslim groups. One of the first African American-led Muslim movements was the Moorish Science Temple (MST), established in Chicago in 1925 by Timothy Drew. (Some authors have mistakenly dated the founding of the MST to 1913, when the same man founded the Canaanite Temple in Newark, New Jersey.) Drew taught that African Americans were actually Moors, or natives of Morocco. Their race was not black, colored, or Negro—words that Drew detested—but Asiatic. Like all other Asiatics, which included the entire nonwhite world of South America, Africa, and Asia, Moors were by nature Muslims, he said.

Drew, who changed his name to Noble Drew Ali, established the Moorish Science Temple to bring Moors back to their original religion, create a sense of community separate from whites, develop self-respect and self-love, follow a strict moral code, and encourage spiritual development. His followers believed that he was a prophet. The presence of the word "science" in the name of his organization indicated that Drew Ali, like other advocates of what was called "New Thought" in the 1920s, believed in the mystical sciences that could close the gap between the material and spiritual worlds. Human beings, he said, could improve their health, their wealth, and other aspects of their worldly existence through meditation, prayer, and other spiritual practices.

In 1927, he published his *Holy Koran of the Moorish Science Temple*, a scripture entirely different from the seventh-century Qur'an. This sixty-four-page text included some of Drew Ali's original teachings on the origins of Moors but was filled mainly with reprinted selections from other mystical texts—the same kind of literature that Alexander Russell Webb and followers of the theosophy movement would have read. These selections described how to train the mind to seek a higher state of spiritual being and advocated strict control of the body as a means to cleanse the soul.

The Moorish Science Temple, which still exists in a few different institutional forms, eventually spread to several other cities and even small towns such as Mounds City, Illinois. Known for its colorful pageantry, the organization adopted many of its Islamic symbols from the Black Shriners, or the Ancient Egyptian Arabic Order of the Nobles of the Mystic Shrine, a fraternal organization that named its lodges after famous figures in Islamic history, used the Turkish fez as its official headgear, and staged large parades along the streets of black America. Moorish men wore the fez and the turban and female members donned ceremonial veils. In addition, the Moors publicly performed

Moorish dramas, including one in which Noble Drew Ali promised to be hung with a rope and to heal the sick. In several cities, the Moors manufactured toiletries and herbal remedies to raise funds and spark interest in the faith. Their product line included Moorish Mineral and Healing Oil, and Moorish Body Builder and Blood Purifier, which was a tonic for "rheumatism, lung trouble, rundown constitutions, indigestion, and loss of manhood."

In the late 1930s or early 1940s, the African American anthropologist Arthur Huff Fauset observed a Friday evening prayer service at the Moors' Philadelphia temple. He noted the quiet, contemplative nature of the service. Participants chanted a hymn called "Moslem's That Old Time Religion" to the tune of "Give Me That Old Time Religion." They also read the holy scripture of their prophet and were reminded of the importance of their name, their national origins, their religion, and their great Asiatic history in Canaan, Egypt, and Morocco. Followers extended their arms in a salute and prayed: "Allah, Father of the Universe, the father of Love, Truth, Peace, Freedom, and Justice. Allah is my protector, my Guide, and my Salvation by night and by day, through His Holy Prophet, Drew Ali. Amen." The words they recited and the gestures they used were different from those of most other Muslims, but the Moorish Science Temple represented an important moment in the history of Islam in the United States. It was the first example of an independent, African American Muslim missionary group devoted to the cause of spreading Islam, however defined.

The Moors were not the only indigenous African American Muslim group to form in this gestational period for American Muslim institutions. In 1930, the mysterious Wallace D. Fard, or Farad Muhammad, established the Nation of Islam in the Wilderness of North America. As Fard peddled silks and other wares door to door in the black neighborhoods of Detroit, he proclaimed the same message that the Ahmadi missionaries and the Moorish Science Temple had broadcast a few years before in the Roaring Twenties. The original religion of the black people, he said, was Islam, and their original language was Arabic.

One of his chief lieutenants, Georgia migrant Elijah Poole, saw in Wallace D. Fard what Ahmadi followers saw in Ghulam Ahmad. Poole believed that Fard was the Christian Messiah and the Islamic Mahdi. But Poole went even further. He also declared that Fard was God in the flesh, and he, Elijah Poole of Georgia, was the Messenger of God—doctrines that most other Muslims would find unacceptable. Muhammad also revealed original prophecies about the beginning and end of the world.

Black Muslims, Elijah Muhammad taught, were the first people of the earth, whose beautiful way of life was upset when a mad, evil scientist named Yacub genetically engineered a race of white devils. These white people eventually enslaved black people, converting them to Christianity and bringing them to the New World. But God had not abandoned his people, said Muhammad. Appearing in the person of Wallace D. Fard, the Almighty selected him, Elijah Muhammad, to mentally resurrect black people and lead them back to Islam, after which they could confidently await a coming apocalypse in which God would destroy the white devil and the black man would once again rule the earth.

After Fard inexplicably disappeared in 1934, Poole struggled with other members of the Nation of Islam for leadership of the group. Poole, who eventually took the name Elijah Muhammad, moved to Chicago and led the Nation of Islam's Temple No. 2. During World War II, the federal government prosecuted Elijah Muhammad as a draft dodger and a traitor. The Federal Bureau of Investigation, which conducted extensive surveillance on black American organizations after World War I, feared that African American Muslim groups were potentially radical. In the years leading up to World War II, Director J. Edgar Hoover was particularly scared of a potential "colored" alliance between the Japanese empire and African Americans. Elijah Muhammad was convicted only of failing to enlist in the armed services, and was sent in 1943 to a federal prison in Milan, Michigan.

During this time, his wife, Clara Muhammad, sustained the Nation of Islam, visiting her husband in prison, carrying messages back and forth, and helping to coordinate temple activities—all the while raising her eight children. Too little is known about her role or that of other women during this era. Women were clearly present and central to the growth of movements such as the Moorish Science Temple and Nation of Islam, but their story remains largely untold. Because of their absence in histories about the early black Muslim groups, it is sometimes assumed that these movements appealed largely to men. The many photographs of female Muslims from the 1920s and 1930s tell a different story.

Many women may have been attracted to these groups for some of the same reasons that men were. The Nation of Islam appealed to African Americans on many levels simultaneously. It was, at once, a political, a social, and a religious organization. Like some other religious groups of its era, it encouraged the practice of a socially conservative morality, condemning sports, secular entertainment, sexual promiscuity, obesity, tobacco, and other vices. Good Muslims, the Nation of Islam taught, should be clean living—pure, hard-working, punctual, disciplined, and modestly dressed. Children were taught these values in the Nation of Islam's primary and secondary schools. Women in the organization joined the Muslim Girls Training-General

Civilization Class to learn home economics, etiquette, and later, self-defense. Men joined the Fruit of Islam and practiced military drills and various religious catechisms. Men wore bow ties and dark suits; women wore robes and often a head scarf. Both men and women in the movement later testified that these activities made them feel dignified and proud.

Elijah Muhammad preached the need for economic and financial independence, encouraging believers to establish and patronize their own businesses, and he emphasized the need for black political self-determination as well. Teaching his followers that the total separation of the races would be the only lasting solution to racism, Elijah Muhammad told them not to vote in U.S. elections or serve in the U.S. military. They were members of the Nation of Islam, not the United States. Movement temples displayed a special Nation of Islam flag that featured an Islamic crescent, among other symbols.

Malcolm X played a major role in the success of the Nation of Islam. Born Malcolm Little in 1925 in Omaha, Nebraska, he was the son of Earl and Louise Little, both of whom were involved in Marcus Garvey's UNIA. During World War II, the teenage Malcolm lived in both Boston and New York, where he became a part of the zoot suit generation. He avoided the draft, enjoyed a life of dancing and drinking, and became a petty criminal. After he was caught and sentenced to prison in 1946, he came to regret what he described as his hedonistic life-style and converted to Elijah Muhammad's version of Islam. He was paroled in 1952 and quickly rose through the ranks of the Nation, leading organization temples in Boston, Philadelphia, and finally Harlem, in New York City. Though Malcolm X would leave the organization and declare his allegiance to Sunni Islam in the 1960s, most of his career was given to Elijah Muhammad's Nation of Islam.

In the late 1950s, the Nation of Islam became the best-known Muslim organization in the United States. But during the 1930s and 1940s, it was only one of the many such independent black Muslim groups vying for converts to Islam. While both the Moorish Science Temple and the Nation of Islam practiced versions of Islam that would be rejected as un-Islamic by most other Muslims, other African Americans formed specifically Sunni Islamic groups. Sunni Muslims, who account for the majority of Muslims worldwide, are diverse by linguistic group, class, nation, race, and ethnicity. But Sunni Muslims do have in common some basic religious practices and principles. Most affirm the absolute oneness of God and the unique nature of the Qur'an, which is considered to be God's final word revealed to the Prophet Muhammad of Arabia in the seventh century CE. Most Sunni Muslims also share a commitment to daily prayers, fasting during the month of Ramadan, charity, and, if possible, pilgrimage to Mecca once during their lifetimes.

During the 1930s, an increasing number of African Americans became aware of these teachings and devoted themselves to them in varying degrees. In 1939, Daoud Ahmed Faisal, an African American emigrant from the Caribbean, leased a brownstone at 143 State Street in Brooklyn Heights for his Islamic Mission of America. This mosque, which catered to African Americans but also welcomed Muslim immigrants from the Middle East, was located just one block from Atlantic Avenue, the heart of Brooklyn's Arab American community. Though it is not clear where Faisal received his training in Sunni Islamic practice, there was ample opportunity for him to converse with Sunni Muslim visitors, diplomats, and immigrants. His mosque offered Friday congregational prayers, and during the 1940s, Shaikh Daoud, as his followers called him, became a powerful missionary for Islam, advocating the faith as the only true religion for all humankind, regardless of race.

Some converts came to Sunni Islam after first learning about Islam in the Moorish Science Temple. South Carolina migrant James Lomax, for example, joined the Moorish Science Temple in Chicago in the 1920s. After Noble Drew Ali died in 1929, he left the movement and traveled to Cairo, Egypt, where he hoped to learn more about Islam. He also adopted a new Muslim name, Muhammad Ezaldeen, and in the late 1930s established an organization called the Addeynu Allahe Universal Arabic Association. Teaching his followers about the Qur'an, sometimes using the original Arabic, Ezaldeen stressed what he said was the Arab identity of African Americans. His movement spread from Philadelphia to other cities, and around 1940, his followers purchased several hundred acres near Buffalo in West Valley, New York, for the purpose of establishing a self-sustaining African American Muslim community devoted to the principles of Islam.

A June 2, 1946, *Buffalo Courier-Express* article entitled "Mohammedan Village Byproduct of Depression" chronicled the origins of the utopian community. A full-page spread in the newspaper included pictures of African American Muslim males, who wore white turbans and dark fezzes and bowed down on their knees, extending their palms in prayerful repose. Other photographs depicted female members who donned white turbans and posed in front of an unfinished wood building that was to be used as a school and mosque. The forty residents of the community owned a little less than five hundred acres, including farm land. One man, Ebn Muhammad, was pictured herding cows. Many of these African American Muslims claimed that they had Arabic ancestry *and* that they were born in the South or in nearby Buffalo.

A believer named Tahleeb Sayyed explained that Hemlock Hill, as the community was called, began in response to the Great Depression. "Thing were tough and we had a hard time getting along," he said. "So we tried to figure out some plan that would help us provide for ourselves without asking for relief or being oppressed." Believers pooled their money and bought land on which they could live and farm, hoping that they could avoid the fate of so many Americans of all colors who went hungry during this era. Ten percent of each farmer's earnings was supposed to be contributed back to the community. "We hope some day to be almost self-sufficient," said Sayyed. Such independence would allow the believers more freedom to observe their religious duties, including the five daily prayers, he noted. After the United States entered World War II in 1941, the military build-up led to employment opportunities in steel mills and foundries, and some residents used their wages from these factory jobs to build homes in Hemlock Hill.

Though the numbers of African American Muslims living in the West Valley community declined in subsequent decades, the history of this largely forgotten experiment helped to establish important precedents in American Islamic history. Like thousands of other Americans of various faiths, twentieth-century African American Muslims would go on to create agrarian communities in which Islam could be practiced in bucolic and peaceful settings. The origins of the community as a part of the Addeynu Allahe Universal Arabic Association is also a reminder of the various early paths by which African Americans became Sunni Muslims in the first half of the twentieth century.

Other African American Muslims became Sunni Muslims in this era via the Ahmadiyya movement. In St. Louis, Walter Gregg, a Texas native, converted to Islam under the tutelage of African American Ahmadi leader Ahmad Din, or P. Nathaniel

Johnson. Taking the name of Wali Akram, Gregg moved to Cleveland, where he helped to lead the Ahmadi mosque. In 1937, Wali Akram left the Ahmadiyya movement and established his own First Cleveland Mosque. Like other African American religious institutions, the First Cleveland Mosque performed multiple functions, both secular and sacred. In addition to its religious mission, Akram's organization repeated Marcus Garvey's call for black economic independence from white markets and encouraged blacks to organize politically. Akram, like most African American Muslim leaders, regardless of sectarian orientation, believed that Islam and the Arabic language were the proud heritage of African Americans. A critical mass of followers in Cleveland agreed, and sustained a Sunni mosque devoted to Akram's teachings.

In the early 1940s, some of the country's most prominent African American Muslim leaders, including Wali Akram, Muhammad Ezaldeen, and Daoud Ahmed Faisal, attempted to form an organizational umbrella, the Uniting Islamic Societies of America. During the 1943 All Moslem and Arab Convention in Philadelphia, Akram presented a draft constitution for the group. By the time the second convention was held in 1944 in Pittsburgh, however, the constitution had still not been approved. The movement to unite all of these African American groups into one association withered.

But the growth of Islam among African Americans continued. By the end of World War II, thousands of African Americans had adopted Islam as their religious identity. The fact that Muslims were associated with the politics of protest against white supremacy was a source of Islam's popularity among blacks, as was Islam's association with economic self-determination. But these were not the only reasons why African Americans wanted to become Muslims. While many African American

Muslims shared some sense of Islam's positive political and economic potential, they were also attracted to Islam for religious reasons.

As P. Nathaniel Johnson's conversion to Ahmadiyya Islam in the 1920s demonstrates, many African Americans thought that Islam offered a convincing theology and a rational argument about the nature of God. Some of them considered the Qur'an to be the most scientific and accurate of all the world's great sacred scriptures. Others believed that Islam was a mystical science whose religious secrets, once unlocked, would set them upon a path of good health, upstanding morals, economic well-being, and deep spirituality. Some forms of Islam practiced in black America, like that of the Moorish Science Temple and the Nation of Islam, bore little resemblance to anything Islamic from abroad. Others kinds of Islam, like Inayat Khan's Sufism and African American Sunni Islam, were American adaptations of Islamic traditions from South Asia, the Middle East, and Southeastern Europe. The very adaptability of Islam in the hearts of people who called themselves Muslims led to the faith's remarkable flowering during this era. If African slaves had been the first practitioners of Islam in the United States, African American Muslims who lived in the first half of the twentieth century helped to establish Islam's institutional longevity in America.

This 1924 article by African American Muslim leader Ahmad Din illustrates how some black Americans were attracted to Islamic religion because of their belief in the Qur'an as God's revelation to humankind. Ahmad Din, born P. Nathaniel Johnson, uses botanical imagery to describe the Qur'an as the most vibrant of world's scriptures. He also praises the Prophet Muhammad, who revealed the Qur'an, as a master spiritualist, invoking the idea that Muhammad was the communication medium that linked human beings to God.

In the field of religious literature Mohammed's Koran is the healthiest plant with the hardiest stalk, produces the sweetest bloom and yields the more wholesome fruit.

The soil which gave to it healthy growth was rich beyond comparison. Allah's abundance made its foliage green, its blossoms beautiful, and its yield so heavy that whosoever reaps has but to enjoy an everlasting harvest.

This plant of which I speak, grew from the true seed to maturity; no grafting on of other plants, no artificial irrigation, no pruning to make it trim was necessary, this plant—QURAN!

Other plants in the field of religious literature? Let us review them. Their seeds were true but ah! look at them now! How sad! Much deliberate meddling has been done.

Perusing a certain Holy Book I found it to be a plant withered, barely being kept alive by artificial watering not at all green—dying! This book, The Torah—Talmud of Judaism. I perused another Holy Book and it was found to be a plant faded, green stems and a few green leaves from true vines grafted on to give it the appearance of life. This book, The Vedas of Hindoos.

The perusal of another Holy Book found it to be a plant already dead from too much pruning. This book, The Gospels. Besides these, some others I perused, finding them all decadent (Al Quran) excepted.

The Sun of Tradition glowed dimly down through the clouds of Mythology, the atmosphere was dry, the rainbow hung westward on the horizon signifying also that the life-giving rains had passed. Blasted Gardens! But the Prophet's Quran stood as a lone apple tree among the other trees of the garden. Consider the Holy Prophet and his Koran. Take the sent One all in all, what he was, what he accomplished, and the good he inspired others to do. Compare him with all other poets, law-givers, prophets, sons of God, statesmen, etc.; and the son of Abdallah alone stands above all other men that mankind has call "GREAT."

Other bibles are mostly the works of an aggregation of poets, prophets, prophetesses, statesmen and lawgivers, historically covering thousand of years, crammed full of conflicting statements. The Koran comes straight from the mouth of the man who proves himself to be the "MASTER MIND" of the earth.

The Quran is a poem, a code of laws, a prayer book, and the world's best bible combined. THE MAN UNIQUE! THE BOOK UNIQUE! As in a looking glass we behold the MASTER SPIRITUALIST of the world intoxicated with the gifts of God.

O, ye howlers and spillers of ink! Climb Mount Sinai and swim the river Jordan, baptize yourselves in pools of blood, rattle the dry bones in Ezekiel's valley, but the echo of it all is dead after all allowance is made.

CHAPTER THREE

Twentieth-Century Muslim Immigrants: From the Melting Pot to the Cold War

Mary Juma arrived in Ross, North Dakota, in 1902. Like most immigrants who traveled to the United States during the first decade of the twentieth century, she did not come from a country in northern or western Europe. In this period, the majority of immigrants hailed from eastern and southern Europe. But Mary Juma and her husband, Hassin, were not from Italy or Russia. They were from Syria, then a part of the Ottoman Empire. Following the lead of other immigrants who sought riches in America, they sold all of their possessions, asked relatives to take care of their two daughters, and pledged their small farm as collateral for the loan they needed to pay for their travel from Lebanon to France and then to Montreal, Canada. Though many European and Middle Eastern immigrants in this era entered the United States through Ellis Island in New York, others came via Canada. After arriving in Montreal, the Jumas went first to Nebraska and then settled in North Dakota.

Like many of the twenty-six million immigrants who settled in the United States between 1870 and 1920, the Juma family struggled at first to make ends meet. Hassin was a peddler, traveling great distances along railroad tracks, rivers, and roads to sell nearly anything that would fit in a large peddler's pack on his back. In 1902, the Juma family filed a homestead claim to some acreage in North Dakota, where they eventually found ample room on the prairie to create a new life for themselves as Americans. These Syrian American sodbusters bought a horse and plow, cleared the land, planted crops, and raised chickens and cows. In 1903, Mary and Hassin had a son named Charles. Though Mary spoke only in Arabic to her boy, he went to school and learned English. Mary had received no formal education in the old country, and she never learned to read or write, either in Arabic or in English. Nor did she ever learn to speak English. Her son, Charles, acted as translator when necessary.

On the North Dakota prairie, Mary Juma preserved Islamic religious traditions. "Syrians," as they referred to themselves, would gather at her home for Friday congregational prayers. They also fasted during the month of Ramadan. During that time, she recalled later, Syrian immigrants frequently visited each other's homes, and there was a great deal of feasting. When her husband died in 1918, he was buried in a Muslim funeral service. Some Muslim Americans in Ross also butchered their meat according to Muslim dietary guidelines, making the meat *halal*, or permissible. Mike Abdallah, who arrived in Ross in 1911, explained in a Depression-era oral history interview that "an animal should not be shot or hit in the head...it should be bled to death. We think that when an animal is shot or hit in the head, the evil and sins remain in the meat."

Eventually, members of the Ross community established a Muslim cemetery and in 1929 or 1930 they built a mosque, a half-basement building with a shallow gabled roof. *Al-Bayan*, an Arabic language newspaper published in New York, asked its readers to help the residents of Ross complete the modest building. This mosque did not have a place for ritual washing. Instead, congregants bathed before arriving there. The mosque, heated by a coal stove, had no minaret or any other architectural detail that indicated Middle Eastern influence. Constructed out of concrete and wood beams, it might have been mistaken for a one-room school, a small church, or even a storehouse. Muslim men and women prayed in one corner of the building, facing east toward Mecca. They wore hats or caps as they prayed in Arabic on prayer rugs they brought from home.

When a funeral was held outside the mosque, a special shaykh, or religious teacher, would sometimes come from Canada to conduct the services. Men and women prepared the body for burial according to Islamic religious tradition, wrapping the body in a white shroud. Mourners, especially elderly women, would weep and sometimes moan as the body was laid to rest. The tomb would be marked with a gravestone, often containing Arabic writing.

Mary Juma and Mike Abdallah were members of an unusual community. Most of the Ottoman emigrants who arrived in the United States from the 1880s through World War I were Christian. One early historian of the Arab American community estimated that less than 10 percent of the total population was Muslim. But North Dakota was different, at least in the first two decades of the twentieth century. Approximately one-third of all Syrian and Lebanese North Dakotans during this time was Muslim, and more than one hundred Muslims lived in Ross alone.

In the 1930s and 1940s, however, the number of self-identifying Dakotan Muslims declined. A 1930s drought forced many farmers out of business and they moved away. In World War II, many Muslim men and women left to serve in the U.S. armed forces or war industries, and did not return. Some who did remain in North Dakota began joining local Christian churches. Mary Juma's son, Charles, attended the local Lutheran church. Many second-, third-, and fourth-generation Arab Americans in North Dakota stopped identifying themselves as practicing Muslims altogether. Their Islamic identity melted away as they became more and more integrated into their predominantly Christian towns and villages.

American Muslims on the North Dakota prairie were not the only Muslim immigrants who chose to give up their Islamic religious identities. The fate of Islam among some early immigrants from South Asia was similar. Muslims began to arrive from British India, which today includes the nations of India, Pakistan, and Bangladesh, in the nineteenth century. Men from the Punjab, a region in the northwestern section of the Indian subcontinent, settled in Imperial Valley, California, where they generally married Mexican American women, and in all but a few cases did not pass along Islamic religious identity to their children. Elsewhere in the United States, South Asian Muslim sailors, mainly from the country known today as Bangladesh, arrived in port cities such as New Orleans and New York. These Bengali Muslim men were part of the British merchant marine, hired to stoke the fires of coal-burning steam ships that transported cotton and hemp from Bombay and Calcutta to ports around the world. They also worked on passenger ships as servants, deck hands, and cooks.

Sometimes deserting their ships, they disembarked in Great Britain and the United States, where they married and settled down. These immigrants became permanent residents and eventually U.S. citizens. Around 1882, a Bengali man named

Alef Ali arrived in the port of New Orleans. In the 1890s, he married an African American woman with whom he had two daughters. Sometime after the turn of the century, Ali turned his home into a boarding house. Twenty-one other Indian men were living at his address by 1910. These men followed in the footsteps of an earlier generation of Bengali immigrants, peddling dry goods, perfumes, and other "fancy goods." Eventually, these New Orleans residents spread out to other cities in the South and headed north as part of the Great Migration.

Joining more than one and a half million other black migrants who moved from the South to cities such as Detroit, Chicago, Cleveland, Philadelphia, Newark, St. Louis, and New York between World War I and World War II, these Bengali Muslims settled in neighborhoods of color, the so-called ghettoes of northern cities. Their children, who were given names such as Bahadour, Rostom, and Roheamon, were often classified as "colored" or "Negro" on various government documents. In New York, they joined a growing Bengali Muslim community. An increasing number of Bengali sailors was also settling in New York, living in various parts of the city such as the Lower East Side of Manhattan, Harlem, or Hell's Kitchen. Many of these Bengalis married black and Latina American women and put down roots in the nation's largest city.

One of these men was Ibrahim Choudry, a Harlem resident who married a Puerto Rican woman, had children, and, in 1943, became director of the British Merchant Sailor's Club for Indian Seamen. The club served thousands of Indian-style meals to sailors and offered its rooms for both prayer and recreation. Choudry greeted men on the docks, oversaw Friday prayers, coordinated various Muslim holiday celebrations, and staged musical performances at the club. In 1946, he helped Habib Ullah, a Bengali immigrant friend, open one of the first

Indian restaurants in Harlem. Habib Ullah, who also married a Puerto Rican woman, catered parties that combined Indian food and salsa music. He shopped the stores of Spanish Harlem's La Marqueta in order to find the right ingredients for his own special curry, the spice blend used liberally in South Asian cooking.

In this cultural mix, some Bengali Muslim Americans did not always raise their children to practice Islam. Some, such as Habib Ullah, feared that Islamic religion and Bengali language would make his children stick out in the predominantly African American and Latino American cultures of which they were part. Others, such as Ibrahim Choudry, taught their children to pray every day. Choudry's son later remembered that his father would stop during roads trips, ask him to perform the *adhan*, or call to prayer, and pray along the side of the road. In many instances, whether the children of these men prayed or not, they often observed Muslim dietary rules, fasted during the month of Ramadan, and feasted on Eid al-Fitr, the holiday that marks the end of Ramadan. Some of their Latina and African American spouses converted to Islam, while many others did not.

While these South Asian sailors, peddlers, restaurateurs, and entrepreneurs supported the establishment of national and ethnic organizations such as the Pakistan League of America, many of them did not create explicitly religious institutions and associations for other people of South Asian descent. Like the Muslims of North Dakota, by the second and third generation many of them practiced Islam, if they practiced it at all, as individuals and families rather than as communities. When Islamic religious practice was observed in communal settings, it was often to mark a holiday or the passing of a community member. For some, the practice of Islam disappeared completely.

But it would be wrong to conclude from these examples that the Muslim immigrants of the late nineteenth and early twentieth centuries did not establish self-sustaining religious institutions. Arabic-speaking immigrants were settling in American cities around the country and often created religious institutions in those places. During the early 1900s, Syrian and Lebanese Muslims arrived in Quincy, Massachusetts, where they formed community groups devoted to religious and ethnic life. In Michigan City, Indiana, a local Muslim organization formed as early as 1907, and by 1924 this group called itself the Modern Age Arabian Islamic Society. In Cedar Rapids, Iowa, the group that eventually called itself the "Mother Mosque of America" rented space for prayers in 1925, and moved into a newly constructed space in 1934. In Seattle, Washington, a group of Druze, a religious community from the eastern Mediterranean with a complicated and sometimes troubled relationship with other Muslims, may have established a local group in 1907. By the 1920s, this organization, in Arabic called the "First Fruit of the Druze," had developed multiple chapters around North America.

In early twentieth-century Chicago, Bosnian Muslim Americans created a mutual aid society, one of the oldest of its kind among Muslim Americans. These Bosniacs, as they were known in the Windy City, purchased a cemetery, paid one another's hospital bills, and coordinated the celebration of Muslim holidays. Unlike the Syrian and Lebanese immigrants, Bosnians were not speakers of Arabic, and they created their own lively ethnic subculture, often centering on the venerable Ottoman institution of the coffeehouse, where people would spend hours and hours in conversation.

In Detroit, Muslim immigrants were attracted to the employment opportunities available at the growing Ford Motor company. In 1916, the company counted 555 Arabic-speaking men among its employees. Around 1920, the nascent Muslim community in Detroit, like the Bosnians of Chicago, established a mutual aid society to provide burial plots for Muslims. In 1921, two Syrian immigrant brothers, Muhammad and Hussein Karoub, spearheaded the effort to create a Sunni mosque. By the late part of this decade, internal differences and financial difficulties led to the closure of this mosque, but Lebanese and Syrian immigrants, including the Karoub family, continued to create new ones.

Arab American Muslim mosques in Detroit also came to reflect the religious diversity of Muslims from Syria and Lebanon. In Dearborn, near the southeast corner of town where Ford Motor developed its gigantic Rouge plant, immigrants first launched a Sunni mosque and soon thereafter a Shi'i mosque called the Hashemite Hall, named after the Arabian clan from which the Prophet Muhammad had come. Like other Shi'a, who represent 10 or more percent of the worldwide Muslim community, these Arabic-speaking Muslims shared a belief that a member of the Prophet's family was the rightful heir to community leadership after Muhammad. Though they practiced many of the same ritual requirements of their Arabic-speaking Sunni cousins, Shi'i Muslims from Lebanon and Syria also observed special holidays such as Ashura, which commemorates the 680 CE martyrdom of Husayn, the grandson of the Prophet Muhammad and son of Ali, at the hands of a Sunni leader.

Detroit was also a center of Albanian American Muslim activity. In 1912, Albania, the small, Muslim-majority European country located opposite the boot of Italy across the Adriatic Sea, declared its independence from the Ottoman Empire and was subsequently invaded by Greece. Some Albanians, especially from the south of the country, sought refuge in the United

States, first immigrating to New England and then making their way to the Midwest. This first wave of Albanian immigration continued until 1925, the year after which the U.S. Congress passed the National Origins Act. This immigration law severely curtailed immigration from "non-Nordic" countries, favoring immigrants from northern and western European countries. But various exceptions were made to the law, and even when its immigration quotas were enforced, immigrants from non-Nordic countries often found a way to enter the country illegally. After World War II, when Communists took control of Albania, a second wave of Albanian immigrants, often strongly associated with anticommunist politics, came to the United States.

In 1945, at the end of World War II, the Albanian American Moslem Society was formed in Detroit, and in 1949, the Albanian American community established a Sunni mosque. This mosque, like many churches and synagogues, was more than a place for prayer. It was also a space for forming business relationships, making marriages, and discussing politics back in Albania. Just as important, the mosque became a place in which parents hoped to pass on their Muslim religious identity to their children. In 1949, the Albanian American Moslem Society hired Imam Vehbi Isma'il, an Albanian religious teacher who had received his religious credentials in Egypt, to lead the congregation. The imam conducted funerals and weddings, oversaw the Friday congregational prayers, and encouraged community members to participate in the Islamic holidays marking the end of Ramadan and the end of the hajj. He also edited a journal called the *Albanian Moslem Life*, which contained articles in both English and Albanian.

Albanian American Muslims in the Detroit area also founded a Sufi lodge or center, called a *tekke*. In 1953, several families pooled their financial resources to buy a farm southwest of Detroit where a Sufi leader, Baba Rexheb, would take up residence. Baba Rexheb was a celibate spiritual master associated with a particular group of Sufis called the Bektashi order. He was trained, like many religious leaders in the Ottoman Empire, in the Qur'an and in Arabic, Persian, and Turkish languages and literatures. He was also qualified to perform various Sufi ceremonies, including *dhikr*, or remembrance of God, which in the Bektashi order includes the recitation of religious poetry.

At the tekke, Baba Rexheb celebrated holidays that are central to the Bektashi sacred calendar, including the New Year's celebration of Nevruz and the commemoration of Ashura. During Ashura, hundreds of Muslims would come to the tekke to observe the martyrdom of Husayn, the grandson of the Prophet Muhammad. During this sacred time, Muslims who participated in the event might fast, pray, read sacred Turkish texts, and meet for a huge communal feast. The initiates of the Bektashi order, those formal students who had committed themselves to developing a closer relationship to God with the guidance of Baba Rexheb, would participate in a special ceremony marking the actual day of Husayn's death. Despite the fact that these Bektashi Muslims venerated the family of the Prophet Muhammad, they were not Shi'i Muslims—in fact, many Albanian American Muslims in Detroit would attend the Sunni mosque in town and also visit the Bektashi tekke.

The presence of Albanian American Muslims, their Sunni mosque, and their Bektashi tekke illustrates just how ethnically and religiously diverse Muslims American immigrant communities had become by the middle of the twentieth century. During this time, immigrant American Muslims established religious networks, often along ethnic lines, that were national in scope. In 1952, approximately twenty mosques in North America formed the Federation of Islamic Associations (FIA) in the United States and Canada. Arab American in origins, the FIA soon incorporated Muslim immigrants from other ethnic backgrounds into its activities. It sponsored summer camps for young Muslim Americans and staged a popular annual convention. During the annual meetings, which rotated among various cities, members taught one another about various aspects of Islam, prayed together, debated the state of U.S. relations to Muslim states abroad, and frequently danced in the evenings to the sounds of Middle Eastern music and the Carlos Rivera Orchestra.

Increasingly, these Muslim American immigrants and their children, like the African American Muslims of the 1920s and 1930s, were fashioning an American Islamic faith that reflected their own needs, interests, and identities. Unlike the disappearing Muslims of North Dakota and the Bengali father who feared that Islam would stigmatize his son, these Muslims held on to their religious identities. But they also crafted an Islam that celebrated American patriotism and cultural integration. There was no better example of this phenomenon than the Islamic center of Toledo, Ohio, also called the American Moslem Society, which encouraged its members to be active U.S. citizens and proud Muslim practitioners. Operating like many American churches and synagogues, this mosque offered its congregants opportunities to develop business ties within the community, socialize with one another, and organize cultural events.

In 1959, Abdo Elkholy, an Egyptian Muslim sociologist who taught at Northern Illinois University, studied this community as part of a research project funded by the Dodge Foundation, a prominent American social science institution. Elkholy concluded that there was a strong connection between the practice of Islam in this mosque and what he termed "Americanization." Muslims who actively participated in mosque activities, he argued, were more likely to assimilate into middle class American culture than those who did not. Such findings contradicted the assumptions of some social scientists, who thought that "foreign" religions such as Islam prevented strong identification with American values and beliefs.

But how did the mosque encourage Muslim immigrants to identify with white, American middle-class values and behavior? Like many sociologists, Elkholy first examined the occupation and income level of mosque members, attempting to link the mosque's middle-class values to the class identity of its members. He discovered that many of the people who went to the mosque were middle-class business owners. Although the consumption and sale of alcoholic beverages is prohibited by Islamic law, a number of these Muslims owned bars and liquor stores. In fact, 127 of Toledo's 420 bars were owned by Muslims. Like other members of the American middle class in the 1950s, these bar-owning Muslims believed that upstanding American citizens should be members of a religious community. In 1955 they used some of their liquor profits to build a mosque for the Toledo community.

Elkholy explained their support of the mosque as a way to purify their liquor money. He assumed that these Muslims were motivated at least in part by "subconscious religious guilt," though the bar and liquor store owners themselves did not admit to feeling guilty about their occupations. Elkholy also asserted that Muslim involvement in liquor-related businesses was a sign of Americanization. But this interpretation ignored the fact that temperance, or total abstinence from alcohol, was itself a mainstream American value. If immigrants wished to assimilate into Anglo-American Protestant Christian culture, they may have been as likely to avoid alcohol as to consume or sell it.

There is another explanation for the seeming incongruity of Muslims who both owned bars and supported their local mosque. The Syrian-Lebanese Americans who lived in Toledo may have been practicing Muslims, but they were not scholars of the shari'a, or Islamic law and ethics. Liquor, though condemned by religious scholars, had been a part of Arabs' everyday lives since the Middle Ages, when Middle Eastern Muslims pioneered the distillation of alcohol and gave it its name—the English word alcohol is derived from an Arabic word. Temperance may not have been broadly accepted as an absolute requirement of Muslim American identity until later, perhaps in the 1960s and 1970s.

Whatever the reason, Toledo's Muslims were focused on other concerns and values in the 1950s. "To be a good Moslem you have to be a good American and vice versa," said a female teacher at the mosque's Sunday school to Elkholy. Echoing the ecumenical views of many middle-class Jewish and Christian Americans in the 1950s, this teacher explained to her Toledo students that Islam recognized the validity of other faiths, supported the brotherhood of all, and opposed discrimination based on language, nation, or race. Many members of the mosque agreed, arguing that Islamic religion is a universal faith that has always adjusted to the particular cultures in which it has been practiced. One second-generation Muslim told Elkholy that "Islam in America...has to take into account the particular features of the American culture. It has to be a living thing in our everyday life and it has to contribute its share to the culture surrounding us."

For many mosque-goers, embracing their Muslim American identity also meant being open to interfaith marriages. Some male and female second-generation members at the time were married to non-Muslim, often white Christian spouses. These spouses were invited to participate in the life of the mosque without having to convert to Islam, although many of them did eventually become Muslims. While believers maintained that integrating Islam into American life required certain shifts in traditional practice, they also claimed that these innovations strengthened the faith of Muslim American practitioners.

The mosque strove to involve men, women, and children in its activities. At the time of Elkholy's study, about 150 students, aged 4 to 15 years, attended the Sunday school each week. At noon, the children, separated by gender, would line up behind the imam to perform the congregational prayer. Children also attended Arabic school on Thursday evenings, and twice a month they met in a youth club sponsored by the FIA. Though women were not formal leaders of the mosque, their contributions were essential to its success. Only women taught in the Sunday school, and the mosque's Ladies Auxiliary sold tickets to mosque dinners, made Middle Eastern pastries, and put on community picnics. According to Elkholy, the mosque could not have functioned without their commitment and hard work.

In many ways, these particular Muslim Americans had achieved the American dream. The stigma of their immigrant background had been transformed into a strong sense of religious and ethnic identity that helped them to become, at least in their local circumstances, American, white, and middle class. Proud of their ethnic heritage, they also considered themselves to be true American patriots. Unlike those Muslim immigrants who let go of their religious identities, these Americans found a way to reconcile their faith with the pressures of social, political, and cultural assimilation.

But at the same moment that second- and third-generation Muslim Americans such as the Toledo mosque-goers and the Albanian American Society celebrated their American national identities, the meaning of American patriotism was changing to reflect new political realities. Over the next few decades, it would become more and more difficult for Muslim American immigrants to express unreserved support for the U.S. government, especially its foreign policy. After World War II, the United States emerged as the preeminent global military and economic power, challenged only by the Soviet Union. In meeting the military and political threat posed by the Soviets, President Harry S Truman's policy was to contain Soviet influence in other countries and to amass a preponderance of power—that is, to gather so much economic, political, and military strength that no other nation could possibly challenge the United States as world leader.

The United States and the Soviet Union entered the era of the Cold War. Struggling for political influence around the world, these nations pressured countries in Africa and Asia, most of whom had just declared their independence from their former European colonial masters, to take sides in the conflict. Asian and African leaders such as Prime Minister Jawaharlal Nehru of India, President Sukarno of Indonesia, and President Gamal Abdel Nasser of Egypt resisted such pressure, pleading for the right to remain neutral and focus on the economic and social development of their countries. But remaining neutral was difficult as both the Soviets and the Americans attempted to influence the regional and domestic politics of the developing world. After Prime Minister Mohammed Mossadeq of Iran nationalized his country's oil assets, seizing them from a British-controlled company, U.S. President Dwight D. Eisenhower agreed to help Great Britain overthrow the democratically elected leader in 1953. Such interventions generated anger toward U.S. foreign policy among many Asians and Africans, including Muslims.

In the Middle East, regional events would also lead many Arabs, including Muslims, to oppose U.S. foreign policy. The creation of the state of Israel in 1948 and the subsequent Palestinian refugee crisis resulted in opprobrium toward the Israelis and sympathy for the Palestinians among Arabic-speaking people and Muslims around the world. For many Muslims and non-Muslims in the "third world" of Asia and Africa, Israel was an anomaly and a symbol of European colonialism. While Israeli Jews argued that they, like other oppressed groups, deserved their own nation, many non-Jews in the Middle East and beyond felt that the Israelis had stolen the land of the Palestinians in order to create a nation for themselves.

Then, in 1956, the Israeli, British, and French takeover of the Suez Canal in Egypt provoked further outrage. Fearing that this military action would upset the balance of power between the United States and the Soviet Union in the Middle East— and angry that he had not been consulted before the move— President Eisenhower ordered these countries to leave. After an armistice was reached, Egyptian President Nasser, a military officer who had helped to overthrow the British-backed Egyptian monarchy in 1952, declared victory. Nasser became an international symbol of Arab national self-determination and resistance to neocolonial interference in the newly independent states of Asia and Africa.

Nasser also became a hero to many African Americans, who increasingly linked their struggle for civil rights to the independence of people of color abroad. When Nasser hosted an Afro-Asian conference in 1958, Elijah Muhammad telegrammed the Egyptian president to assure him that "freedom, justice and equality for all Africans and Asians is of far-reaching importance, not only to you of the East, but also to over 17,000,000 of your long-lost brothers of African-Asian descent here in the

West." Some members of the Nation of Islam hung Nasser's picture in their homes. Nasser was received enthusiastically by Muslims and non-Muslims alike when he visited Harlem in 1960. Malcolm X saw in Nasser the strong leadership needed to help Africans and people of color more generally control their own economic and political future.

But Nasser was not a hero to all. In consolidating his power over the nation of Egypt, he had repressed the voices not only of the old colonial elites, but also of members of an organization called the Muslim Brothers. A political party and religious organization, the Muslim Brothers dreamed of a world that would be governed by the principles of the Qur'an, the Sunna, or the traditions of the Prophet Muhammad, and the *shari'a*, or Islamic law and ethics. They were "Islamists" who believed that Islam was both a religion and a state, a complete way of life. With Nasser's brand of socialist and nationalist politics stirring the cauldron of revolution across the Middle East, leaders of other states, particularly Saudi Arabia, identified the Muslim Brothers and other Islamists as allies in the struggle against the growing power of Nasser and his revolutionary ideals.

During the 1950s and 1960s, a new wave of Muslim immigrants came to American shores, and some of them brought critical attitudes toward U.S. foreign policy. Many of the immigrants were Palestinian refugees who had been displaced in 1948 or Arab students looking to further their educations. Some of them were Islamists, formal members of the Muslim Brothers or individuals who supported the idea that Islam could be a solution to the political, social, and cultural problems of the world. In 1963, several Muslim students formed the Muslim Students Association at the University of Illinois, Urbana-Champaign. Among the founders were three Muslim Brothers.

Like Christian missionaries in the United States, these students and their allies distributed missionary literature, established organizations devoted to their cause, and spread the good word in their neighborhoods. They challenged the legitimacy of Muslim American groups, including the Nation of Islam and local mosques such as the American Moslem Society of Toledo, who were, in their eyes, either theologically incorrect or insufficiently pious. In 1962, a Dartmouth student, Ahmed Osman, traveled to a Nation of Islam meeting at Mosque No. 7 in Harlem to spar with Malcolm X over Elijah Muhammad's admittedly unorthodox teachings about Islam. During the question and answer period of the temple meeting, Osman challenged the religious legitimacy of the Nation of Islam. Malcolm X defended Elijah Muhammad, but also seemed to be intrigued by the student's critique—after Osman sent Malcolm X some religious literature from the Islamic Center of Geneva, Malcolm apparently requested additional materials.

Muslim missionaries from the Islamic world had been reaching out to African Americans since the 1920s, encouraging them to convert to Islam. But Malcolm X presented a special challenge and opportunity for Islamist missionaries in the 1960s. There was no more powerful symbol of Islam in America at the time than Malcolm X, and immigrant and foreign missionaries targeted him for conversion to their form of political Islam. When Malcolm X declared his independence from Elijah Muhammad and the Nation of Islam in March 1964, these missionaries had an opportunity to develop closer ties with him. Malcolm turned for counsel to Mahmoud Youssef Shawarbi, an Egyptian professor of Islamic studies who was also a community leader among immigrant Muslims.

Shawarbi encouraged Malcolm to make the hajj, talked to him about the core teachings of Sunni Islam, wrote a letter of introduction intended for Saudi authorities, and gave him a copy of *The Eternal Message of Muhammad*, a book by Islamist author Abd al-Rahman Azzam. When Malcolm arrived in Saudi Arabia for the hajj, he telephoned Azzam's son, who was married to a daughter of Saudi prince Faysal. Soon, Malcolm became a guest of the Saudi state, and after his pilgrimage he would even meet Prince Faysal himself. Later that year, Malcolm returned to Saudi Arabia for formal training as a Muslim missionary under the guidance of the secretary general of the World Muslim League, a Saudi-supported missionary organization that spread the message of Islamism around the world.

The hajj was a spiritual turning point for Malcolm X, as he came to see Islam as a religion that could heal the wounds of racism in the hearts of human beings and transcend all racial divisions. He wrote to his community of followers in New York saying that he had felt kinship with his fellow pilgrims, "who were of all colors.... We were all participating in the same ritual, displaying a spirit of unity and brotherhood that my experiences in America had led me to believe never could exist between the white and the non-white." During his pilgrimage, Malcolm even shared food and drink with a blue-eyed white Muslim, declaring that racism could be overcome with the help of almighty God. Malcolm credited Islam with opening his eyes to the essential equality of all human beings.

At the same time, Malcolm X did not relinquish his commitment to black liberation politics. Even on the hajj, Malcolm continued to talk with other Muslims about the "evils and the indignities that are suffered by the black man in America." At a July 27, 1964, speech in Cairo, he explained that he would always have the dual burden of being a religiously active Muslim and a politically active African American: "My fight is two-fold, my burden is double, my responsibilities multiple...material as well as spiritual, political as well as religious, racial as well as non-racial." Anticipating the calls for black power that would become popular after 1966, Malcolm emphasized the need for black people to create and control the organizations that would liberate them from economic and political oppression. Whites could help blacks achieve their liberation by eliminating discrimination, he said, but they should not expect to be invited to join all-black organizations. Malcolm declared that black unity was a prerequisite to any multiracial political movement, and he became a strong advocate of pan-Africanism, the movement to unite people of African descent in a common struggle for political, economic, and cultural self-determination.

Some immigrant Muslim Americans and foreign Muslim missionaries challenged Malcolm X's continued focus on black issues. In response, Malcolm explicitly rejected the notion that Islam, which he viewed as a religious rather than a political system, could solve the social and political problems of black people. Those problems, he said, went beyond religion. When Said Ramadan, the director of the Islamic center in Geneva, pressed him in a 1965 interview about his commitment to racial politics, Malcolm defended his political activism. "As a Black American," Malcolm wrote, "I do feel that my first responsibility is to my twenty-two million fellow Black Americans who suffer the same indignities because of their color as I do."

But Muslim missionaries from abroad were successful in convincing some African Americans that Islamic religion could provide a political solution to racism. At Daoud Ahmed Faisal's State Street Mosque in Brooklyn, New York, Pakistani missionary Hafis Mahbub was appointed to teach the Qur'an. Young African American Muslim men, including the poet Sulaiman al-Hadi, studied with Mahbub. Mahbub frequently led the early-morning prayer at the mosque and preached that Islam was a

Fig. 1: Captured in West Africa around 1730, Job Ben Solomon was brought to British North America as a slave, traveled to Great Britain as a free man, and returned to his native Senegal in 1735.

Fig. 2: In the 1820s, Omar ibn Sayyid (c. 1770–1864) was celebrated by white Carolinians as an African convert to Christianity, though he may have secretly continued to practice Islam until his death.

Fig. 3: Omar ibn Sayyid, an African American Muslim slave literate in Arabic, rendered Sura an-Nasr, the Chapter of Help, from Qur'an 110:1–3, c. 1857. These verses may be translated as follows: "When the help of God comes and the victory / and you see people joining the religion of God in crowds / Recite the praise of your lord and pray for God's forgiveness / He is always ready to forgive."

Fig. 4: Alexander Russell Webb, former U.S. consul to the Philippines and the first prominent white American Muslim convert, spoke on behalf of Islam at Chicago's Parliament of Religions in 1893.

MOORISH SCIENCE TEMPLE of AMERICA
OCTOBER 15. 16. 17. 18. 19. 20. 1928
PROPHET NOBLE DREW ALI. FOUNDER

Fig. 5: Members of the Moorish Science Temple, the first nationwide African American Muslim organization, with founder Noble Drew Ali (first row, standing, fifth from left), in 1928 outside the group's Chicago headquarters. Ali's Islamic teachings and symbols, including his Napoleonic salute in this picture, were inspired by the Black Shriners, an African American fraternal organization.

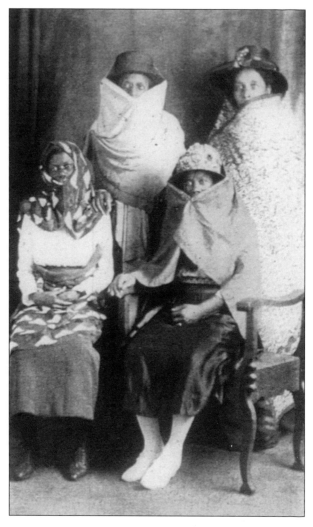

Fig. 6: African American women have been converting to Islam since the 1920s. These women, who were members of the Ahmadiyya movement of Islam, donned both stylish hats and colorful veils to cover their hair.

Fig. 7: The Islamic Center of Washington, DC, was dedicated in 1957. Mosques in the United States include Middle Eastern-style structures, converted storefront churches and Jewish synagogues, and modernistic buildings based on complex geometric patterns. This mosque combines Egyptian Mamluk, Ottoman Turkish, and other traditional architectural elements from the Islamic world.

Fig. 8: Malcolm X, an iconic figure of the 1960s, was at the center of national debates about civil rights and black power. First a member of the Nation of Islam, he declared his allegiance to Sunni Islam in 1964.

Fig. 9: Muhammad Ali, the heavyweight boxing champion of the world and a member of the Nation of Islam, looks on as his teacher, the Honorable Elijah Muhammad, addresses a crowd in 1964. After refusing to be drafted into the U.S. armed forces during the Vietnam era, Ali was stripped of his boxing title.

FRONT ROW: Sandy Terpsidou, Hasan Masood, Beverly Bradley, secretary; Linda Clark, president; Saeed Nizami, religious chairman; Ainuddin Shaikh, H. B. Jacobini, adviser. SECOND ROW: Iraj Mansouri, Arshad Karim, Abdus Sattar Ahmad, Abdul Lateef, Habib Akhter, Afak Haydar, Said Anabtawi, treasurer.

Moslem Students Assoc.

One of the important events of the year for the Moslem Students Association was the observance of Romadan, an Islam season of prayer and fasting from sunrise to sunset between January 14 and February 14. The end of the period was marked by the Eid with a large dinner and celebration. The group produces a monthly newsletter, "Bilal," and holds weekly prayer sessions in the Center. This year, Dr. William A. Harris of the Philosophy Department discussed "Islam and Race."

Fig. 10: Members of the Southern Illinois University chapter of the Muslim Students Association, pictured in the 1966 SIU yearbook, were from diverse racial, ethnic, and national backgrounds. The chapter, which was led by Linda Clark, a white woman, conducted weekly Friday prayers, produced a monthly newsletter, and celebrated Ramadan on the Carbondale campus.

Fig. 11: Selling everything from hot dogs to apple pies, Midamar Halal Foods of Cedar Rapids, Iowa, is one of many Muslim-owned food suppliers that follow Islamic dietary rules.

Fig. 12: Muslim American children who trace their roots to Jordan, Morocco, and Syria play outside Madrasa Tul Ilm, or the School of Knowledge, in Indianapolis, Indiana, in 2008. The number of Muslim American parochial schools multiplied dramatically in the late twentieth century.

complete way of life. He told members of Faisal's congregation that they should live in expectation of the coming Islamic order and exile themselves from mainstream society, which was corrupt and un-Islamic. Their movement eventually became known as Dar al-Islam, or the House of Islam.

In addition to spreading the message that Islam could provide a solution to the woes of society, many of the recent immigrants and foreign students also called on Muslim Americans to practice Islam's religious rules more strictly. This dynamic was often present wherever second- and third-generation Muslim Americans encountered newly arrived Muslims, as the story of the Islamic Center of New England in the 1960s illustrates. The seven Syrian-Lebanese families who helped to establish the community in the first half of the twentieth century, like many of Toledo's Syrian-Lebanese immigrants, sought to create a mosque that performed the same functions as American churches and synagogues. They were also worried by the fact that their children could not read the Qur'an or say their prayers in Arabic.

When their organization, the Arab American Banner Society of Quincy, Massachusetts, set out in 1961 to build a new mosque, they engaged in fundraising activities typical of American congregations. Though the community received a $5000 grant from King Saud, who visited Boston for an eye operation in 1961, the bulk of their funds came from American sources. They raised money from their non-Muslim neighbors and associates by holding raffles, staging card games, holding auctions, and, most important of all, inviting the public to a large annual picnic, at which, reportedly, it was possible to purchase alcoholic drinks. In 1963, construction of the mosque began. Still faced with the problem of insufficient funds, the members of the mosque arranged to finance the mosque by taking out a mortgage. Though this mortgage violated a traditional Islamic prohibition against paying and charging interest, the community had no other way to pay its construction bill.

The dedication of the new mosque in 1964 drew a large crowd, including local Christian leaders, politicians, Muslim visitors from other states, and the head of the FIA. The featured speaker for the event was Muhammad Jawad Chirri, a prominent Muslim leader from Detroit. Once settled into its new home, the community not only offered congregational prayers and educational programs, but also Halloween parties and sock hops. Over the next ten years the number of members would triple.

By the late 1960s, the newly arrived immigrants and students had assumed leadership positions in the mosque, and they sought to eliminate any practices that they considered to be religiously improper. Alcohol and gambling were banned. The Ladies' Auxiliary replaced these fundraising activities with dinners, lunches, bake sales, and bazaars. The new immigrants and foreign students taught second- and third-generation Muslims how to perform their prayers in Arabic, often teaching them phonetically. They also translated literature about Islam into English and offered lectures on Islamic religious traditions.

What was happening at the Islamic Center of New England in the 1960s was the beginning of a trend. In the last three decades of the twentieth century, newly arrived immigrants would play an important role in sparking various religious awakenings among Muslim Americans. These awakenings were spurred partly by the changing politics of Muslim American identity in the 1960s. Whereas many Muslim American immigrants had stressed their ethnic and national origins as a primary source of identity in the first half of the twentieth century, during the era of the Cold War and the conflict in Vietnam, they increasingly turned to religion to define their identity. The use of U.S. power abroad transformed Muslim American consciousness at home. Many Muslim Americans of various racial and ethnic backgrounds questioned the morality of the United States and its allies, including Israel, Iran, Saudi Arabia, and South Vietnam.

When combined in the 1970s with concerns about the sexual revolution, the Watergate scandal, the economy, and other domestic issues, this distress over U.S. foreign policy led some Muslim Americans, like Christian Americans, to conclude that the world could be saved only through a massive religious revival, or at least a return to religious values. For some, the religious awakening of the late twentieth century inspired the hope that the Muslim community in the United States would become a beacon for the rest of the Islamic world, modeling what Islam could be if lived with verve and commitment. Though it was highly diverse in form and content, the revival also united Muslim Americans in the belief that their destiny was shared.

In 1939, Works Progress Administration employee Everal McKinnon interviewed North Dakota resident Mary Juma as part of the Federal Writers Project to study the disappearing ethnic cultures of Americans. Juma described Muslim life on the North Dakota prairie, preserving the memory of a community that has largely disappeared.

I was born in Byria, Rushia, Syria. I don't know my exact age, but according to my naturalization papers, I am sixty-nine years old. I am sure that I am at least seventy-five years of age, however. My home in Syria was a large, one-story, stone house....

My religion in the Old Country was Moslem....I received no education, as our people figured that it was a waste of time and money to teach a girl to read and write. There were no schools in our village, and those that were taught to read and write, were taught by a tutor....

The people in our vicinity were migrating to America and kept writing back about the riches in America. Everyone wanted to move and we were a family of the many that contemplated leaving....

In 1902, we came to western North Dakota where we started to peddle. It was at the time when there was such an influx of people to take homesteads, and for no reason at all, we decided to try homesteading too.

We started clearing the land immediately, and within a year, had a horse, plow, disk, drag, and drill. We also had some cattle and chickens. When there was a very little work to do on the farm, my husband traveled to Minnesota and eastern North Dakota to peddle.

In 1903, my son, Charles, was born. He was the first Syrian child born in western North Dakota. We were the first Syrians to homestead in this community, but soon many people from that country came to settle here.

Our home has always been a gathering place for the Syrian folk. Not many parties or celebrations were held, except for occasions like a wedding or such. Before we built our church [mosque], we held services at the different homes. We have a month of fasting, after which everyone visits the home of another, and there was a lot of feasting....

We always speak in our native tongue at home, except my grand-children who won't speak Syrian to their parents. They do speak in Syrian to me because I cannot speak nor understand English. My grand-children range from fourteen months of age to eight years, and there are four of them....

There is too great a comparison to say much about America and my native land. This country has everything, and we have freedom. When we pay taxes, we get schools, roads, and an efficiency in the government. In the Old Country, we paid taxes and Turkey took all the money, and Syria receiving nothing in return. We were repaid by having Turkey force our boys to join her army. The climate in the Old Country was wonderful, but we [Americans] have such a climate down south.

If I had my life to live over, I would come to America sooner than I did. I would have liked to visit the people in Syria five or ten years ago, but now that I am helpless, I wouldn't care to go. I don't ever want to go back there to live.

CHAPTER FOUR

Religious Awakenings of the Late Twentieth Century

On October 3, 1965, President Lyndon B. Johnson signed a new immigration law called the Hart-Celler Act. Speaking from Liberty Island in New York, President Johnson stressed that the new legislation was not "revolutionary." He claimed that it would "not restructure our daily lives." On this particular point, Johnson would turn out to be at least partially incorrect. Part of a wave of civil rights legislation that emerged from the U.S. Congress in 1964 and 1965, this new law enacted radical changes in immigration policy that affected the social fabric of the United States. The Hart-Celler Act expunged the racist immigration quotas that had been established under the National Origins Act of 1924 and the McCarran-Walter Act of 1952. Under the old system, limits on immigration had favored white people: the annual quotas allowed 149,667 Europeans, 2,990 Asians, and only 1,400 Africans to come to the United States. The new law changed that, banning discriminatory quotas based on national origins.

As a result, millions of nonwhite people, including Muslims from Asia and Africa, immigrated to the United States over the next several decades. From 1966 to 1997, approximately 2,780,000 people immigrated to the United States from areas of the world with significant Muslim populations. Because the U.S. government did not ask about people's religious affiliations on the U.S. census or record that information on immigration documents, it is not known exactly how many of these immigrants were Muslim. One demographer estimates that approximately 1.1 million immigrants were Muslim. Of those, about 327,000 came from Arabic-speaking countries in North Africa and the Middle East, while approximately 316,000 arrived from the South Asian countries of India, Pakistan, and Bangladesh. Still others were from Iran, sub-Saharan Africa, Southeastern Europe, Turkey, the Caribbean, South America, Canada, and Southeast Asia.

One of these immigrants was Fazlur Rahman, an Islamic studies scholar who in 1968 accepted a post as a visiting professor at the University of California, Los Angeles. Born in 1919 in the Indian Punjab, Rahman completed a college degree in British India and then traveled to Oxford University, where he earned a doctorate, writing his thesis on the medieval Islamic philosopher Ibn Sina. In the 1950s, Rahman taught Islamic studies both at the University of Durham in England and at McGill University in Montreal, Canada. But in 1962, he was appointed head of the Institute for Islamic Research in Karachi, Pakistan, where he turned his scholarly eye toward public affairs. Committed to the idea that Islam was a religion geared not only toward personal piety but also toward social ethics, Rahman bemoaned the lack of God-consciousness in modern human society and government.

After the 1964 elections, Rahman became an adviser to Pakistani President Ayyub Khan. But when a new political regime came to power in the late 1960s, Professor Rahman fell into disfavor. Controversial because of his interpretation of the Qur'an and the *hadith*, the reports of the sayings and deeds of the Prophet Muhammad, Rahman also held liberal political positions that were unacceptable to some social conservatives. He received violent threats from his political opponents. Although many of the Muslims who immigrated to the United States during this period came in search of economic opportunity, Rahman was one of those who sought to escape the political turmoil of his home country. For Rahman, the United States became the location of a self-imposed exile.

After spending the 1968–1969 school year in Los Angeles, Rahman was offered a permanent post at the University of Chicago. Until his death in 1988, he trained graduate students in Islamic studies and conducted research. He also became a public intellectual, effectively advocating his interpretation of Islamic religion for both Muslim and non-Muslim audiences in the United States. Even though many American Muslims eventually rejected his conclusions, Fazlur Rahman's approach to the sacred scriptures captured the spirit of the age.

Rahman believed that all human activity was subject to God's authority and must be performed in accordance with God's commands. On this point, Rahman's voice sounded similar to that of many of his socially conservative Islamist opponents in Pakistan, who proclaimed that Islam was not only a private religion, but also a public way of life. The Qur'an, they all agreed, was a revelation that offered pertinent moral solutions to the social, political, and economic problems of the world.

But Rahman's approach to the Qur'an differed from that of many Islamists—and from the approach of more traditional interpreters of Islam. Much of his reinterpretation of Islamic tradition concerned the ways what Muslims read their sacred scriptures. Rather than focusing on the piecemeal, line-by-line interpretation of the Qur'an, as many of the great Qur'anic commentators had done, Rahman contended that the Qur'an must be understood as one coherent text. Every single verse of the Qur'an should be read, he said, with knowledge of what every other verse of the scripture says. He also declared that Muslims should use the Qur'an as an interpretive key to understanding the *hadith*, the reports about the words and actions of the Prophet Muhammad, rather than using the *hadith* as an interpretive key to understanding the Qur'an. This approach was revolutionary, and drew opposition from both defenders of Islamic tradition and Islamists.

Even more, Rahman said, the Qur'an must be interpreted with regard to the historical contexts in which it was revealed. According to Rahman, examining the time and place in which each verse came to the Prophet Muhammad was necessary to understanding its general meaning. "The Qur'an," he wrote in *Islam and Modernity* (1982), "is the divine response, through the Prophet's mind, to the moral and social situation of the Prophet's Arabia." Once readers analyzed the ways that qur'anic revelation was geared toward seventh-century Arabia, they could then extrapolate the general principles of the Qur'an, and apply those general principles to their own historical circumstances.

In Rahman's hands, and those of many other American Muslim interpreters, this style of interpretation led to ethical conclusions dramatically different from those prescribed in the *shari'a*, or Islamic law and ethics. Take, for example, the idea that men can marry up to four wives. Rahman argued that this interpretation distorted the Qur'an's emphasis on justice, equality, and the need for a healthy relationship between a man and a woman. Delving into all of the qur'anic verses that had a bearing on the issue of polygamy, he proclaimed that earlier scholars of Islam simply misread the text. On this basis, Rahman declared that the true Islamic position on marriage favored monogamy.

Rahman's approach to qur'anic interpretation directly influenced the religious thought of other Muslim Americans, especially those who later became part of the global Islamic feminist movement. Amina Wadud, an African American Muslim scholar, for example, adopted Rahman's style of interpretation in her popular book, *Qur'an and Woman: Rereading the Sacred Text from a Woman's Perspective*. Born Mary Teasley in 1952, Amina Wadud grew up in Washington, D.C., the daughter of a Methodist preacher. She took an Islamic name after becoming a Muslim in the 1970s. In preparation for her Ph.D. in Islamic studies from the University of Michigan, she studied Arabic in Egypt. Wadud then applied her training in Islamic studies to an innovative reading of the Qur'an and its view of women.

In *Qur'an and Woman*, Wadud asserted that the Qur'an regards men and women as completely equal, if also different and complementary. The Qur'an, she wrote, opposes any social hierarchy based on gender, and does not prescribe fixed social roles for women. Women are free to be homemakers, wives, and mothers, but they need not perform any of these roles, according to Wadud's reading of the Qur'an. Islamic societies, she noted, are traditionally patriarchal, but not because of the Qur'an. Instead, she claimed, men in these societies had applied their biases against women in their interpretations of the Qur'an. Because men generally held more power in these societies, she stated, their interpretations obtained the force of law and custom.

Some Islamic feminists in Muslim-majority countries became familiar with her work before some American Muslims did. Between 1989 and 1992, Wadud was an instructor at the International Islamic University in Malaysia, where she became a member of Sisters in Islam, Malaysia's leading women's rights organization. Her book, *Qur'an and Woman*, was first published in 1992 by a Malaysian press and then in 1999 was republished by Oxford University Press. In 1994, she gave a presentation during the Friday congregational prayers at the Claremont Main Road Mosque in Capetown, South Africa, challenging the traditional understanding that only men were to give such addresses during Friday prayers. A little more than a decade later, on March 18, 2005, she led both male and female congregational prayers in New York, violating what even most moderate Muslims considered to be an absolute prohibition on women leading mixed-gender congregations in prayer. Because no mosque would host the event, the prayers took place at the Cathedral of St. John the Divine, an Episcopalian church.

Many American Muslims in the last three decades of the twentieth century—and the first decade of the twenty-first century—thought that Amina Wadud and some other Islamic feminists had simply gone too far, too fast. But what these people shared with Amina Wadud and Fazlur Rahman was a real commitment to discovering the true meaning of their sacred scriptures and then applying those understandings to their daily lives. Whether they were socially conservative or liberal, an unprecedented number of Muslim Americans during this period came to believe that they must read the scriptures for themselves. Like many other people of faith in the modern era—from Hindus to Christians—Muslims emphasized the importance of literacy for the purpose of directly encountering the sacred scriptures without the help of an intermediary.

This orientation toward the Qur'an represented a shift in Islamic religious tradition. For most of Islamic history, the majority of Muslims had experienced the Qur'an as an oral and aural text, a scripture that should be literally recited and heard. To be sure, religious scholars had long studied the interpretation of the written Qur'an. But they represented a minority. Most experienced the sacred scriptures in a way that was true to the literal meaning of its title—Qur'an literally means recitation. Although many American Muslims in this period took an interest in Qur'an recitation, both listening to and learning to chant the verses of the Qur'an, they also read the Qur'an in a new light. By the late twentieth century, most American Muslims treated the Qur'an—and the Sunna—as something to be studied, as they would study a textbook.

This was as true in African American circles as it was in immigrant circles. In 1975, when Elijah Muhammad died, he left his son, Wallace D. Muhammad, or W. D. Mohammed, in charge of the Nation of Islam. After taking the reins, Mohammed changed the religious doctrines and political outlook of this historically African American movement and aligned it with Sunni Islamic tradition. Born in 1933, W. D. Mohammed had been exposed as a teenager to Sunni Islam through Palestinian and Egyptian teachers at the University of Islam, the Nation of Islam's primary and secondary school in Chicago. As early as 1958, he introduced his own Qur'an-based teachings to Nation of Islam members in Philadelphia. When he was finally introduced as the movement's new leader at the annual Chicago convention on February 26, 1975, it was clear that a change was coming.

In the following years he debunked the idea that his father was a prophet like Muhammad, the charge that white people were blue-eyed devils, and the belief that W. D. Fard was God. He introduced the U.S. flag into Nation of Islam mosques, changed the name of the organization to the World Community of al-Islam in the West, and negotiated a contract to supply ready-made meals to the U.S. government. By the 1980s, he frequently delivered lectures on the compatibility of Islamic religion with personal freedom, individualism, and democracy, asserting that these values were Islamic in nature. Mohammed grounded all of his teaching in the Qur'an and the Sunna, the traditions of the Prophet Muhammad. He advised his followers not to rely on him, but to rely on the Qur'an.

Not all of his followers accepted such changes, which led to a split in the movement in 1978. Minister Louis Farrakhan, who had become national spokesman for Elijah Muhammad after Malcolm X left the Nation of Islam in 1964, rejected W. D. Mohammed's radical reforms. Farrakhan reaffirmed his belief in the prophecy of Elijah Muhammad and the divinity of W. D. Fard. Though there were other claimants to Elijah Muhammad's religious legacy, Farrakhan became the most prominent of them. Calling his new organization the Nation of Islam, he set about rebuilding the movement.

But Minister Farrakhan did not take over the mosques aligned with W. D. Mohammed and he did not inherit many of W. D. Mohammed's followers. Despite press reports to the contrary, it is clear in retrospect that W. D. Mohammed's identification with Sunni Islam attracted new members to his movement. Like other African American Muslims in the late twentieth century, they were convinced that religious truth lay in the sacred sources of Islam. Within two decades of W. D. Mohammed's reforms of the Nation of Islam, both his male and female members were meeting in informal study groups to interpret the Qur'an and the Sunna for themselves.

In early 1990s Los Angeles, for example, anthropologist Carolyn Rouse discovered scores of African American Sunni women at mosques aligned with W. D. Mohammed who were studying the scriptures in their search for a closer relationship to God and guidance for daily living. These women regularly met in homes and at local mosques to discuss the Qur'an and the stories of women's lives in seventh-century Arabia, debating their meaning for contemporary society. They tackled issues such as the unfaithfulness of men, divorce, domestic violence, and the wearing of *hijab*, or a head scarf. Their ongoing dialogue often had an effect on the way men in the community, including imams, came to interpret Islam's teachings on gender relations and women's issues. Some men became open to changing their behavior toward wives or female congregants based on the religious arguments of women.

In the 1990s, the Internet also became a forum in which American Muslims of various racial backgrounds debated the meaning of their sacred scriptures. Muslims did not need a degree in the Islamic religion or a professorship at a distinguished Islamic university to issue *fatwas*, or religious opinions, on the World Wide Web. Participating in various on-line dialogues, American Muslims logged on by the thousands and became part of a global, English-language cybercommunity of Muslims. To be sure, the Internet could be used to spread intolerant interpretations of the Qur'an and Sunna, as groups such as Usama Bin Ladin's al-Qa'ida demonstrated. But most online interpreters of the Qur'an and the Sunna did not share in al-Qa'ida's venom, instead using the Internet to debate the qur'anic worldview on everything from Islamic business ethics to personal etiquette.

Pakistani American Muslim author and activist Asma Gull Hasan participated, for example, in an e-dialogue about dating and premarital sex. Hasan's comments appeared on an e-mail distribution list hosted by the Muslim Public Affairs Council in Los Angeles. Responding to another member's condemnation of dating, Hasan stated that dating does not necessarily lead to sex. Dating, she wrote, could provide companionship, which may or may not lead to marriage. Yes, she agreed, there was a prohibition against dating in traditional Islamic interpretations of the Qur'an and the Sunna. But she retorted, not unlike Fazlur Rahman or Amina Wadud, that the teachings of the Qur'an and the Sunna must be understood in their historical context. "In the Prophet's time, 1,400 years ago in Arabia," she wrote, "people married at the age of fifteen anyway because they only expected to live to the mid-30s." There must be a way, Hasan pleaded, to live out the moral vision of the Qur'an and have healthy relationships with people of the opposite sex.

As these remarks begin to show, the Muslim religious awakening under way in the United States during the last decades of the twentieth century had many faces. In addition to producing new readings of the Qur'an and Sunna, Muslim Americans of various ethnic, linguistic, class, sectarian, and racial backgrounds sought to adhere more zealously to the ethical requirements of their religion. Although there were political components to the American Islamic awakening, this revival was largely religious in tone and content. Like American Christians who sought to "get saved from the Sixties," many American Muslims in the 1970s and 1980s emphasized personal piety and individual responsibility as pathways to large-scale social reform. Some American Muslims doubted that the government could solve what they viewed as moral problems.

During this era, American Muslims focused more intently on observing the pillars of Islamic practice, including daily prayers, the giving of charity, the dawn-to-dusk fast during the month of Ramadan, and the hajj, the annual pilgrimage to Mecca. Idris M. Diaz, for example, set out to make the pilgrimage to

Mecca. The son of a Honduran father and an American mother, Diaz first became interested in Islam in the late 1960s. Still an elementary school student, Diaz noticed well-dressed members of Elijah Muhammad's Nation of Islam selling the *Muhammad Speaks* newspaper in his neighborhood of Jamaica, Queens, in New York City. He admired the Nation of Islam's business ventures and its struggle against drug use in the black community, but he could not accept the teaching that white people were devils.

Later, after reading *The Autobiography of Malcolm X* and coming to know a group of Sunni Muslims, he officially converted to Islam. It was 1975, and he was a few weeks shy of his sixteenth birthday. Diaz attended Wesleyan University and then Columbia School of Journalism, eventually landing a job as a reporter for the *Philadelphia Inquirer*. In 1988, the paper sent Diaz to Saudi Arabia to cover the hajj.

After checking in at the Sheraton hotel in Medina, Diaz purchased an *ihram* outfit, the white robes generally worn by males on the hajj. A few days later, he set off to perform the pilgrimage rites. At the Grand Mosque in Mecca, he circled the Ka'ba, the small, cube-shaped building that many Muslims believe was originally built by the prophet Abraham. Joining thousands of fellow pilgrims, he ran between the two hills called Safa and Marwa, repeating Hagar's desperate search to find water for her son, Ishmael. After resting a day, Diaz left for Mount Arafat, where he asked God's forgiveness for his sins. There, he passed the time with a group of Egyptian Muslims. Even though the Egyptians could not speak English and Diaz could not speak Arabic, Diaz felt the warm embrace of their hospitality.

During the trip, Diaz met other Muslim Americans who were participating in the hajj. One was Mahfouz Rahman, a Bangladeshi American physician who treated Diaz for a bad foot and a fever. Another was Pittsburgh resident Ishaq Salaam, an African American truck driver who converted to Islam in the 1970s. Salaam was a Mississippi native who had served in the U.S. armed services in World War II. He first became interested in Islam during the 1950s when he heard Elijah Muhammad speak about self-help. After converting to Sunni Islam in the 1970s, he developed the desire to perform hajj. He heard about others in the community of W. D. Mohammed who were making the journey, and he set out to save enough money to do so himself.

The hajj was not an easy trip for this seventy-nine-year-old man, and Salaam's determination, fortitude, and unfailingly sunny disposition inspired the younger Diaz to ignore his own annoyance with the grueling heat and difficult crowds. Diaz made it through the hajj, though he dubbed it a form of Islamic boot camp. Like the other million-plus pilgrims, Diaz completed his hajj with one last walk around the Ka'ba in Mecca. After doing so, he paused, and took stock of the past five days. Looking at the Ka'ba, he cried to God, "This life is Yours! Just *take* it. Wherever You want it to go, I'll be. This is Yours! C'mon! *Just come get me.*"

Such sentiments expressed the feelings of many American Muslims committed to the Islamic awakening of the late twentieth century. Their religious fervor took many forms. In addition to adhering to the pillars of Islamic practice, some Muslim Americans attempted to bring their personal finances in line with what they understood to be Islamic guidelines. They avoided all interest-bearing savings and checking accounts, eschewed mortgage financing for their homes, and sought to invest only in ethical companies.

In 1973, the Muslim Students Association of both the United States and Canada established the North American Islamic Trust, a not-for-profit organization that held the deeds of various mosques and Islamic centers, offered advice on investments that complied with the requirements of the *shari'a*, and distributed Islamic books to people in the United States and beyond. In 1999, the Trust sponsored the creation of the Dow Jones Islamic Market Indices, which listed and tracked companies that, according to an international panel of Islamic legal experts, operated in an ethical manner. Various mutual funds, including the Amana Growth Fund and Dow Jones Islamic Fund, bought the shares of such companies and offered individual retirement accounts and other products to Muslim investors.

In this era of Islamic awakening, many Muslim Americans experimented with different styles of dress to express their religious identities. Some men took to wearing a form of head cover: perhaps a *kufi*, a skullcap that might be made of African kente cloth; a *tarboosh*, a cylindrical, often red hat once popular in the Middle East; or a *kuffiyeh*, an Arab headdress secured by a band around the head. Muslim men also wore full-length robes: the *thobe*, an ankle-length, often white garment, or a *jellaba*, a woolen cloak. Some men donned clothes that celebrated aspects of their cultural heritage: for African Americans, the dashiki, the colorful shirt popular in West Africa; and for South Asian Americans, the *shalwar kameez*, a combination of loose pants and a tunic.

More and more Muslim American women, like Muslim women abroad, chose to wear a *hijab*, a head scarf often sewn from cotton or silk cloth. Some women wore hats or bandanas instead. Some Muslim American women also dressed in loose-fitting, full-length garments, called *jilbabs*. A 2002 article in *Azizah* women's magazine proclaimed that the *jilbab* could be "dressy or casual," floral or plain, a "staple in the wardrobes of many Muslim women" that was fashionable, affordable, elegant, warm, and modest. A few women wore the *niqab*, covering every part of their body but their eyes. But not all Muslim American women were keen on these fashions and modes of dress. Some covered their hair only when making prayers, arguing that this was all that the Qur'an required.

Muslim Americans in this era also focused on the preparation and consumption of food as one of the primary identity markers of their religious observance. New Muslim groceries and butcher shops sprouted up in neighborhoods in which mosques already existed or were newly established. The butcher shops slaughtered animals following the *shari'a* guidelines that make meat *halal*, or permissible, to eat. Instead of shooting, hitting, or electrifying the animal to death, butchers use a sharp knife to cut the animal's neck. The animal becomes unconscious due to a lack of oxygen, and then bleeds to death. Muslim American consumers demanded the option of purchasing *halal* meat for home, and more Muslim restaurateurs prepared *halal* dishes. Muslim restaurants also avoided serving alcohol and pork, both of which are *haram*, or prohibited, by *shari'a* guidelines. In places with a sizable population of Muslim Americans, national fast food chains began to offer *halal* food. Muslim-owned Subway sandwich shops in New Jersey and California earned sales volume awards for doing so.

The demand for Islamically compliant consumer products also led to the development of Muslim-owned wholesale suppliers and mail order businesses. Midamar, established in Cedar Rapids, Iowa, in 1974, sold a whole line of *halal* food products, including pizza toppings, sausage, deli meats, samosas, and chicken nuggets. Such products were advertised in the pages of Muslim American periodicals such as *The Muslim Journal* and *Islamic Horizons*.

Publications funded by various Muslim organizations and mosques, including the North American Islamic Trust, gave

Muslim consumers guidance about what popular consumer products were religiously permitted and prohibited. In 1984, the Islamic Food and Nutrition Council of America published *Islamic Dietary Laws and Practices.* Ten years later, Zaheer Uddin issued his *Handbook of Halaal and Haraam Products*, which categorized more than 5,000 consumer items as either permissible or prohibited. Uddin pointed out that some popular cheeses, for example, contained gelatin or enzymes that were derived from animals not slaughtered according to Islamic guidelines. Popular shampoos, soaps, and toothpastes sometimes contained animal byproducts, including pork collagen.

Some Muslim American governing bodies also launched efforts to certify food products and suppliers as *halal.* The Islamic Food and Nutrition Council of America, for example, developed a formal certification process, published a consumer magazine, and sponsored national food conferences. Based in Chicago, this nonprofit organization began an extensive Web site in 1998 that offered advice on hundreds of consumer products from around the world. As the Internet emerged as a central space for discussion, debate, and learning among Muslim Americans, other sites devoted to food appeared. Zabiha.com became a site for consumer reviews of various restaurants and markets around the world. In addition to rating their adherence to Islamic dietary norms, user reviews included information on the quality and price of the food and the cleanliness of the establishment. All of the details became important in the quest to live a more Islamic life.

In addition to the emphasis on Islam's ethical requirements and a deep interest in learning the Qur'an, the religious awakening of the late twentieth century was also expressed in the growth of various Sufi groups. Historically speaking, Sufism, often referred to as the mystical or esoteric branch of Islamic religion, has included various religious practices meant to bring the believer closer to the presence of God. Taking to heart the Qur'an's frequent injunctions to remember God, Sufi Muslims have developed prayers, breathing exercises and other forms of meditation, dancing, and singing in their quest to achieve a rich, spiritual life. Sufism was by no means new to the United States in the late 1900s, but it did attract more followers, including non-Muslims, during this time. Several Sufi groups, both home-grown and transplanted, developed followings in the United States in the latter part of the twentieth century.

Sufi master M. R. Bawa Muhaiyaddeen, a post-1965 immi-grant from Sri Lanka, created a Sufi fellowship in Philadelphia in 1971. This student of the Qadiri Sufi order cast a wide net for all those devoted to "contemplating the truth and unity of God." He welcomed people of all racial and religious back-grounds to his Sufi center, although the majority of his followers were white Americans. Gradually introducing his followers to the Qur'an and the pillars of Islamic religious practice, in 1981, the shaykh, as a spiritual master in Islam is sometimes called, directed his followers to keep the five daily prayers.

Disturbed by growing frictions between Muslims and non-Muslims in the 1970s and 1980s, Muhaiyaddeen affirmed the inherent worth of all mainstream religions, condemned violence as an ineffective solution to the world's problems, and stressed the need for world leaders to avoid demagoguery. In the book *Islam and World Peace* (1987), published a year after his death, the leader encouraged Muslims to see in the Qur'an not only ethical guidance for daily life, but the very light of God in the world. If believers truly imbibed its contents, he argued, they would see the oneness of all humankind, and the need to offer all people "love, compassion, patience, and tolerance." If Mus-lims practiced peace, he said, "justice will flourish. Love will cut away all enmity. Compassion will cause God's grace to grow in this world, and then the food of faith and the mercy of all the universes can be offered." This message was an attractive one to the several thousand people who sought refuge from an American society torn apart by violence and social divisions.

For some Muslim Americans, the zeal of their Islamic awakening was directed not only inwardly, toward personal ethical and spiritual renewal, but also outwardly, toward the reform of U.S. society. During this period, some Muslims, like socially conservative Christians, believed that American popular culture had become obsessed with illicit sex, drug use, and other libertine behavior. They joined other American religious leaders in calling for a moral revival among people of all faiths. In the early 1990s, the immigrant-led Islamic Center of Southern California in Los Angeles hosted an interfaith forum on sex and morality. Keynote speakers included Roman Catholic Cardinal Roger Mahony, Imam W. D. Mohammed, and Jewish radio personality Dennis Praeger. Covering the event for the *Minaret*, the official magazine of the Los Angeles-based Center, Aslam Abdullah emphasized that American Muslims were ready to help the United States become a more moral nation. "We want to be seen on moral frontiers," said a local imam interviewed for the story. "On abortion, drugs, homelessness and human dignity, we want the message of Islam to be known."

The 1979 Iranian revolution also inspired many Muslim Americans, both Shi'a and Sunni, immigrant and indigenous, to dream of an era when social justice would rule in every part of the globe. For most Iranians, even those who did not support the revolutionary leader Ayatollah Khomeini, the 1979 revolution put a stop to an oppressive and violent regime that was propped up by the American government. For most Americans, the overthrow of the Shah, coming as it did just a few years after the United States withdrawal from Vietnam in 1975, was a terrifying blow. When Iranian students took over the American embassy and kidnapped dozens of embassy personnel, many U.S. citizens also became enraged. Hate crimes against Muslims, Arabs, Iranians, and South Asians rose in the United States.

But such violence did not deter the enthusiasm of many Muslim Americans for the revolution. The Iranian revolution was a symbol of change in Muslim America, and as a symbol, it came to be interpreted in many ways. For Lila and Mohsen Amen, for instance, what started in Detroit as political enthusiasm for the revolution was transformed into a stronger religious observance. Lila, a Sunni Muslim who grew up in Detroit, married Mohsen, a Shi'i immigrant from Lebanon, in 1975. Like many Muslim Americans in that era, they said, they were not very committed to their faith. They often went to dance clubs, stayed up playing cards until three or four in the morning, and did not pray on a regular basis. But after the Iranian revolution, something changed. Many Lebanese American Shi'i Muslims in Detroit hoped for a similar Islamic revolution in Lebanon. "It was a political time," Lila remembered.

This political hope turned into religious zeal. Mohsen went to hear a prominent Lebanese shaykh, Muhammad Husayn Fadlallah, speak in 1981. A large crowd attended. Seeing the old shaykh, whom Mohsen had known since childhood, led him to renew his faith: "It was like somebody shook me and said, 'There is a purpose for you here. You don't [just] work, eat, sleep, and drink and have babies. We are not animals. There is a purpose for you.'" Mohsen started to pray and read the Qur'an more regularly, participated in Islamic study circles, and spent weekend after weekend going to religious events. Lila was at first annoyed, especially since they had children to raise and bills to pay. But eventually, after experiencing a great deal of personal tragedy and illness, Lila also "woke up," as she said, to her faith.

Mohsen and Lila's religious journeys showed that what may have started out as a political commitment turned into a religious commitment. As the new Iranian regime consolidated its political power, its widespread appeal among Muslim Americans as a universal symbol of Islamic justice eventually declined. But enthusiasm for the idea that Islamic religion, if understood correctly, could provide a solution to the social and economic problems of the world did not wane among some Muslim Americans.

Shamim Siddiqui, who immigrated to the United States in 1976, was one Muslim missionary whose openly stated goal was to transform the country into an Islamic state. A former member of Pakistan's Jamaat-i Islami, the political party that supported the implementation of *shari'a* as Pakistan's national law, Siddiqui argued that the United States was the world's best hope for a truly Islamic state. Siddiqui said that the United States is largely democratic, that it is governed by laws, and that at home it supports human rights. But the nation also suffered from a weak economy and even weaker morals. Sounding like some of his evangelical Christian brothers and sisters, Siddiqui identified the source of what he deemed to be America's deterioration: "It lies in denying the authority of the Creator while living on His earth and enjoying His bounties and believing or behaving as if this is the only life and there is no accountability of death."

The solution, he proclaimed, was Islam, which offered Americans "justice, equality, and peace," and a system of "comprehensive guidance for the human society, both in individual and collective spheres." Siddiqui directed Muslim Americans to work within the legal boundaries of the U.S. Constitution. He called on Muslims to use their right to vote, to speak, and to assemble in the effort to transform America into an Islamic state.

The religious awakening of the late twentieth century was indeed suffused with utopian dreams of a better world. But most Muslim Americans did not share Shamim Siddiqui's vision for the country. He failed to become a household name in Muslim America or to convince Muslim Americans that they should fight for the implementation of the *shari'a* as the law of the land. For the most part, Muslim Americans supported the development of Islamic institutions within the existing legal and political frameworks of the United States. To be sure, they wanted nothing less than full recognition of Islam as a legitimate religious "denomination" in the public sphere. This desire was tangibly expressed not only in the pietistic practices of Muslim Americans but also in the growth and development of Islamic institutions, including mosques, schools, and national advocacy groups.

Although accurate numbers are hard to come by, perhaps more than a thousand American mosques and Islamic centers were established in the last three decades of the twentieth century. They appeared wherever groups of Muslims lived—in small college towns, suburbs, and inner cities. By 2000, there was no region of the country without some kind of Muslim mosque.

The architecture of these mosques expressed a variety of styles. Some mosques, like the Islamic Center of Washington, D.C., consciously incorporated the traditional architectural elements of various places of worship in Africa, Asia, and Europe. It incorporated Turkish tiles, Persian carpets, an Egyptian chandelier, Islamic calligraphy, and a tall minaret from which the faithful could be called to prayer. Other mosques, like the headquarters of the Islamic Society of North America, were modern in style, employing geometric details to evoke, but not to imitate, the mosques of the Old World. Many mosques were converted storefront churches or buildings originally built without a religious purpose in mind.

The leadership structure of U.S. mosques was similarly diverse. In some cases, mosques were organized around the authority of a charismatic leader. In many other cases, mosques, like most American churches and synagogues, were run by a board of directors. These boards, often elected by the members, had the power to set mosque policy, manage mosque finances, and hire (or fire) the imam. In most of these mosques, women did not qualify for the position of imam. Like Roman Catholics and Missouri Synod Lutherans, many Muslims said that their tradition did not allow for female preachers (in mixed-gender settings, at least). But women could and did lead mosques as board members or presidents. Chereffe Kadri, for example, led the Islamic Center of Toledo through difficult days after September 11, 2001.

Wherever mosques were built, full-time Islamic schools also appeared. The first national system of elementary and secondary schools was established in the 1960s by Elijah Muhammad. Called the University of Islam and later renamed the Clara Muhammad schools, after the wife of Elijah Muhammad, several dozen Clara Muhammad schools offered children, both Muslims and non-Muslims, an alternative to public education in urban areas. By the 1990s, many immigrant Muslim Americans had followed suit, establishing more than 150 schools across the country.

In Seattle, Washington, Muslim Americans created the Cherry Hill Child Development Center, which followed the Montessori philosophy of education. "Dedicated to the physical, mental, and spiritual health and happiness of the children (ages 3–6) in its care," the school welcomed children of all religious and ethnic backgrounds to attend. Parents, said the school, "should be aware that the religion of Islam pervades the atmosphere of the school," but also promised them that "alternative activities will be provided for children whose parents choose that their children not participate in religious activities." The curriculum included several areas of study: practical life, the sensorial, mathematics, language, Islam, science, geography, history, and art.

As the number of full-time Muslim schools increased, Muslim parents debated whether such parochial schools served the best interests of Muslim American children. Some parents said that separate Muslim schools denied children educational opportunities, ultimately stunting their career potential. Some worried that Muslim children in parochial schools would be isolated from mainstream culture, and argued that sending their children to public school was good preparation for "real life." Others saw mainstream culture as dangerous and unsafe, asserting that Muslim schools were needed precisely to shield their children from violence, unhealthy sexuality, and drugs. In the end, the number of full-time Islamic schools could not accommodate a significant portion of school-aged Muslim Americans, meaning that most attended public schools or looked for alternatives, including charter and private Christian schools.

In addition to building more full-time Islamic schools and mosques, Muslim Americans in this era established a number of important community development and public affairs organizations. In 1982, leaders of the Muslim Students Association came together to establish the Islamic Society of North America (ISNA). ISNA built its headquarters in Plainfield, Indiana, a suburb of Indianapolis, and became a large, multidimensional umbrella group. In addition to staging the largest single annual Muslim American convention, held every Labor Day weekend in Chicago, ISNA offered financial services, religious training, interfaith workshops, and other services to its more than 350 affiliated member mosques and Islamic centers. It also publishes a widely circulated Muslim American magazine called *Islamic Horizons*.

Among the several public affairs organizations founded by Muslim Americans in the late twentieth century, perhaps the most prominent was the Council on American-Islamic Relations (CAIR), established in Washington, D.C., in 1994. Battling anti-Muslim prejudice in the United States, CAIR documented cases of hate crimes against Muslims in the United States, studied the impact of immigration and other laws on Muslims in the United States, and publicized instances of anti-Muslim bias in the news, film and TV, and other mass media. Since 1996, it has issued a report called *The Status of Muslim Civil Rights in the United States* on an annual basis.

Such high-profile public advocacy revealed just how central Islam had become to the public identity of millions of U.S. citizens in this era. Of course, it would be wrong to state that all Muslim Americans participated in some kind of religious awakening in the late 1900s. Some Muslim Americans who traced their roots to Islam one, two, or three generations before simply fell away from the faith. Other first-generation immigrants said that although they were culturally Muslim, they were not practitioners of the religion. Some secularly minded Muslims wanted nothing to do with Islam. But a large number of Muslims, of various racial, ethnic, and class backgrounds, saw new meaning in their religious identity in the late twentieth century. Though they may have disagreed about some of the most basic questions of religious doctrine and practice, these Muslims inhabited a shared universe informed by the hope that Islam would make them better human beings and make America a better place to live.

Asma Gull Hasan, a South Asian American author and blogger for Glamour *magazine, has described herself as a "Muslim feminist cowgirl." In her semiautobiographical book* American Muslims: The New Generation (2000), *she musters her own reading of the Qur'an in waging* jihad, *or struggling with her grandfather over the question of gender equality in Islam.*

I was debating with my extended family once during a family gathering whether Muslim women and men should be allowed to pray in the same room. I reasoned that on Judgment Day men and women will stand equally before God with no gender preference. My grandfather piped up, "No, men are superior in Islam!" We were in my uncle's normally quite noisy Suburban, which had now gone silent at my grandfather's words.

My family members waited a moment, and then said things like, "Oh no!" and "You're in for it now, grandfather!" They were saying all this because I am known in my family for responding vehemently to such statements. I stayed levelheaded, however, and asked my grandfather, "You mean in the Qur'an?"

"Yes!" he said.

"I don't think so," I said.

"No, it says it!" he retorted.

After a few minutes of this yes–no business we finally got to the merits of the argument. My grandfather felt that since God's messengers were all male, men must then be superior in God's eyes. I countered that a woman, Khadijah, Muhammad's wife, was the first convert to Islam. Without her faith in Muhammad, *no Muslims would exist.*

I offered other arguments proving gender equality in Islam, but something told me that my points were falling on deaf ears. I joked that my grandfather must have received the Taliban version of the Qur'an....

Though I tried to make light of the situation, I was saddened that *my own grandfather* would say such a thing, even if he believed it. Does he really think that I, as a woman, am inferior to my brother, merely because he's male? I see in my grandfather the effects of South Asian culture, which is patriarchal, on his interpretation of the Qur'an. Sure, there are a few passages that taken out of context, interpreted from a patriarchal perspective, or not updated for our times (which the Qur'an instructs us to do) imply women's inferiority. They are by no means passages on which to build tenets of Islam, however. When I asked my grandfather to show me where in the Qur'an it says that women are inferior to men, he replied that it would take him some time to find the passage. As he has still not found it, I presume it doesn't exist or isn't clear in its meaning.

But this is what it came to—my own grandfather, a product of his society and prejudices, saying that women are inferior to men. This despite the fact that women outnumber men in his own family. He has five granddaughters and three grandsons—it's in his interest to see women as equal to men! It hurts, but I understand that we all have to read the Qur'an and make our own interpretation. This is my *jihad* with my grandfather.

CHAPTER FIVE

Muslim Americans after 9/11

S etting out to destroy the symbols of U.S. financial, military, and political power on September 11, 2001, nineteen members of al-Qa'ida hijacked and crashed large passenger planes into both towers of New York's World Trade Center and into the Pentagon. A fourth hijacked jet, apparently bound for Washington, D.C., crashed in Pennsylvania. In total, approximately 3,000 human beings were murdered that day. Usama bin Ladin, the leader of al-Qa'ida, considered the attacks to be religiously sanctioned retribution for the suffering caused by U.S. foreign policy in the Middle East. Before and after the attacks, al-Qa'ida members cited several reasons for their violent acts, including U.S.-based support of Israel, the U.S.-led war against Iraq in 1991, the presence of U.S. military bases in the Persian Gulf, and U.S. support for corrupt regimes in the Middle East.

For the families and friends of al-Qa'ida's victims, these attacks resulted in immeasurable loss, deep pain, and anger. For many Americans, including Muslim Americans, the attacks inspired national solidarity in the face of fear and insecurity. After the attacks, for example, some Muslims placed flowers and cards outside of the Muslim Council Center mosque in Washington, D.C., where a large American flag hung in the entrance to the building. In Paterson, New Jersey, Muslims hoisted a banner on Main Street proclaiming that "The Muslim Community Does Not Support Terrorism." All across the country, mosques and Islamic centers flew the American flag and opened their doors to non-Muslims. Muslims sought to educate their non-Muslim neighbors about Islam and reassure the public about their loyalty to the United States and their love of the American dream. Many Americans visited a mosque for the first time, often attending information sessions on Islam in which Muslim leaders explained that Islam is a peaceful religion that does not condone terrorism.

Like so many of their fellow citizens, Muslim Americans also reacted to the attacks with a determination to help the victims. Muslims contributed thousands of dollars to 9/11-related charities. Near Washington, D.C., the All Dulles Area Muslim Society dedicated its Friday congregational prayers to the victims and sponsored a blood drive. Members of the University of Maryland chapter of the Muslim Students Association also gave blood, donated money, and participated in interfaith prayer services for the victims and their families. In Queens, New York, where Pakistani American Mohammad Chaudhary managed a branch office of the Edhi International Foundation, ten-cent garments were sold and donations were accepted for a $10,000 gift to the Red Cross 9/11 disaster relief fund.

All major Muslim American organizations and leaders condemned terrorism and the murder of innocent victims in unambiguous terms. Immediately after the September 11 attacks, the American Muslim Political Coordination Council, which represented the Council of American-Islamic Relations, the Muslim Public Affairs Council, the Islamic Society of North America, and other groups, issued a press release proclaiming that "American Muslims utterly condemn what are apparently vicious and cowardly acts of terrorism against innocent civilians. We join with all Americans in calling for the swift apprehension and punishment of the perpetrators. No political cause could ever be assisted by such immoral acts." Similarly, the Islamic Circle of North America expressed its horror and sadness in the face of such violence, and said that "Islam does not permit such unjust acts." In the following years, Muslim American leaders consistently restated their absolute opposition to terrorism, which they condemned as un-Islamic.

In the immediate aftermath of September 11, Muslim Americans also feared a backlash against them. In the past, some Americans had physically or verbally assaulted Muslims and those who "looked like Muslims" as a reaction to events overseas. After the 1973–1974 OPEC oil embargo of the United States, the Iranian Revolution of 1979, and the 1983 attack on the Marine barracks in Beirut, Muslim Americans had been harassed, beaten up, or threatened by their fellow citizens. After 9/11, President Bush joined American Muslim leaders in asking Americans to protect their fellow Americans, not injure them. On September 17, 2001, he spoke at the Islamic Center of Washington, D.C., declaring, "Those who feel like they can intimidate our fellow citizens to take out their anger don't represent the best of America. They represent the worst of humankind, and they should be ashamed of that kind of behavior."

Alas, such calls went unheeded among some Americans. A few were in the mood for revenge. After Frank Roque was arrested for murdering Balbir Singh Sodhi, a Sikh man whom Roque had mistaken for a Muslim, Roque told Mesa, Arizona, police, "I stand for America all the way. I am an American. Go ahead. Arrest me and let those terrorists run wild." Hours before the crime, according to police, Roque had bragged at a local bar that he was going to "kill the rag heads responsible for September 11."

Perhaps as many as seven people, including an Arab American Christian, were murdered in revenge for 9/11. Other hate crimes included violent assaults against Muslims, attacks against places of worship, and personal harassment. Some Americans told their fellow Muslim citizens to "go back to where they came from" and sent anonymous e-mail messages threatening to kill them. A few Americans actually spat on Muslim American women wearing head scarves. On the whole, anti-Muslim hate crimes in the United States increased 1,700 percent during 2001.

Despite President Bush's strong support for the Muslim American community, many Muslim American leaders asserted that the U.S. government was sending mixed messages about the trustworthiness of Muslim Americans. Using the powers granted to him under the USA Patriot Act, passed in October 2001, U.S. Attorney General John Ashcroft rounded up approximately 1,200 Arab, South Asian, and Muslim men on suspicion of possible ties to terrorism. This was no ordinary law enforcement action. In many instances, the detainees' names were not released, they were not allowed access to a lawyer, and they were held in jail without being charged of a crime. In addition, the FBI sought to interview 8,000 Muslim men to probe their possible connection to or knowledge of terrorism. One Muslim American activist said that these activities sent an important message to non-Muslims: "Most people are probably asking, 'If the government doesn't trust these people, why should I?' "

The foreign policy of the Bush administration also led some Muslim Americans to question the sincerity of President Bush's kind remarks about Muslims and Islam. Although the Muslim American community was divided over the question of whether the United States should forcibly remove the Taliban regime in Afghanistan, some prominent Muslim American leaders supported this military action. Even more Muslim Americans acquiesced to the idea that military action of some kind was inevitable. But the Iraq war of 2003 was different. One poll found that only 13 percent of Muslim Americans supported the invasion of Iraq. Like many non-Muslim Americans, most Muslims pointed out that there was no established link between Saddam Hussein's regime and al-Qa'ida, which was one of the reasons the Bush administration cited in making its case for war. Most Muslim Americans rejected the claim that the Iraq war was a legitimate part of the war on terrorism.

One Muslim American who opposed the Iraq war was hip hop artist and actor Mos Def. Born Dante Smith in 1973, Mos Def was exposed to Islam through his father, who first joined the Nation of Islam and then became a follower of W. D. Mohammed. At the age of nineteen, Mos Def took his own *shahada*, declaring that there was no god but God and that Muhammad was God's messenger. In 1999 his album *Black on Both Sides* established him as one of hip hop's greatest artists and helped to catapult him into a successful acting career. He appeared in television shows, on stage, and in movies, including *Monster's Ball*, *The Italian Job*, and the Emmy-nominated *Something the Lord Made*. He also continued to rap about human rights abuses, black empowerment, and the government's response to Hurricane Katrina.

Mos Def became a harsh critic of the Bush administration's war on terrorism, saying that the threat of terrorism was generally hyped in order to provide an excuse for the war in Iraq and other Bush administration policies. In 2004 he recorded the song, "Bin Laden (Tell the Truth)," with Immortal Technique and Eminem. In it, the rapper accused American politicians of being "professional liars" and proclaimed that "Bin Laden didn't blow up the projects," referring to the World Trade Center. His fellow rapper Jadakiss blamed President Bush for knocking down the towers.

Most American Muslims were not willing to go that far. A 2007 Pew poll found that fewer than 10 percent of Muslim Americans believed that the 9/11 attacks were orchestrated by the U.S. government or a Jewish conspiracy. What Muslim Americans questioned most strongly was the motive behind the war on terrorism. More than half of those surveyed, including 71 percent of native-born, mostly African American Muslim Americans, said that the American-led war on terrorism was not a sincere effort to reduce terrorism.

The U.S. administration contributed to Muslim Americans' negative attitudes about the war on terrorism through its mistaken prosecutions of Muslim Americans as terrorists. Perhaps no case fed the fear of wrongful prosecution and imprisonment more than that of Brandon Mayfield, a white Muslim American attorney from Oregon. On May 6, 2004, the FBI detained Mayfield as a material witness in the investigation of the March 2004 Madrid train bombings that killed 191 people. The FBI claimed that Mayfield's fingerprints matched those of one of the bombers. For nineteen days, the government held him in solitary confinement, subjecting him to what Mayfield later described as "strip searches, sleep deprivation, unsanitary living conditions, shackles and chains, threats, physical pain, and humiliation." But when Spanish authorities publicly announced that the fingerprints belonged to Ouhnane Daoud, an Algerian national, the FBI was forced to release Mayfield. While the Department of Justice vigorously defended its actions in a December 2005 report, it did agree in November 2006 to pay Mayfield $2 million and issue a formal apology for his arrest.

Muslim American leaders also felt that the government was unfairly targeting Muslim organizations, especially charities, as supporters of terrorism. Among these leaders was Laila al-Marayati, a Palestinian American obstetrician-gynecologist and clinical professor at the University of Southern California's School of Medicine. A Muslim philanthropist herself, Marayati was a co-founder of KinderUSA, a charity that provided health care, food, recreational opportunities, and transportation to children in the West Bank and Gaza Strip. As a prominent member of the Muslim American community, she also served as one of President Bill Clinton's appointees to the U.S. Commission on International Religious Freedom and as past president of the Los Angeles-based Muslim Women's League.

Marayati believed that although federal prosecutors had largely failed to win major victories against Muslim American charities, the administration's persecution of these charities would have a chilling effect on Muslim American donations overseas. Even as the Treasury Department lauded its successful closure of Muslim American charities in testimony on Capitol Hill, claimed Marayati, "not a single court case has resulted in a conviction that is related to the events of 9/11 or to al-Qaeda." The government, she said, had succeeded in closing down several charities that were accused of having ties to terrorist organizations. "However," she wrote in a 2005 article in *Pace Law Review*, "no one should be fooled into thinking that America or the American people will be much safer so doing." All they had really done, she declared, was to rack up a political victory at home and to damage U.S. efforts to promote democracy and freedom in the Islamic world.

Although some Muslim Americans focused their social and political activism after 9/11 on issues of war and peace, others voiced the need for reform among Muslim communities in the United States and abroad. Turning inward, they saw 9/11 as a sign of larger problems in the *umma*, the worldwide Muslim community. Ingrid Mattson, a Hartford Seminary professor and Muslim leader who was later elected president of the Islamic Society of North America, argued that "American Muslims have generally been more critical of injustices committed by the American government than of injustices committed by Muslims." Muslims, she said, had the "greatest duty to stop violence committed by Muslims against innocent non-Muslims in the name of Islam." Mattson, a white, Roman Catholic Canadian who converted to Islam in college, denounced "Muslim states who thwart democracy, repress women, use the Qur'an to justify un-Islamic behavior, and encourage violence."

At the same time, she warned that no matter how loudly American Muslims cried out about problems in the Muslim world, their voices would not be taken seriously unless they were "recognized as authentic interpreters of Islam among the global community." American Muslims should not expect, for example, to abandon whatever Islamic religious traditions they disliked and then be greeted with acceptance in the worldwide community. Mattson's reaction to Amina Wadud's leading of the mixed gender prayer in New York in 2005 was thus cautious. She agreed that women were treated like second-class citizens in too many mosques, and she called on women to lead mosques as presidents and board members. But she did not think that female leadership of mixed-gender prayers—an act that defied most Muslims' understanding of Islamic tradition—should be a primary goal in the battle against sexism.

The challenge of being taken seriously by Muslims abroad while also fighting for reform and renewal in Islamic religion was a daunting one. Many self-defined progressive Muslims and Muslim Americans who identified with them argued that the struggle was also necessary. But unlike some other post-9/11 critics of Islam, progressive Muslims were as skeptical about U.S. foreign policy as they were about fellow Muslims. Omid Safi, a Muslim American scholar, reminded other Muslims that they were, as the Qur'an put it, a community in the middle, "calling both Muslims and Americans to the highest good of which we are capable." Being in the middle was not, he said, a "popular or easy place to be." For Safi, an American-born Muslim of Iranian descent, it meant criticizing intolerance and violence among Muslims and non-Muslims alike, opposing elements of U.S. foreign policy, while also advocating for religious pluralism, social justice, and feminism in Muslim communities.

Safi was blunt in his critiques. "Far too long," he admitted, "we have sat silently—I have sat silently—when someone gets up in our Islamic centers, our mosques, and vents poison." He was tired of hearing hate-filled proclamations about "the Jews," the immoral West, and the "corruption of women." At the same time, Safi said that he was disappointed in U.S. support for the Saudi Arabian monarchy and for Pervez Musharraf's coup in Pakistan. Similarly, he would not stay silent in the face of human rights abuses of Muslim prisoners by the U.S. government at Guantanamo Bay. "Let us speak with conviction and compassion, concern and courage, and pray that other like-hearted progressive souls will join this middle community" working for justice everywhere, he wrote.

Even as the initial shock of the 9/11 attacks dissipated, it became clear that Muslim Americans would be in the middle of the war on terrorism whether they liked it or not. Neighbors, co-workers, and non-Muslim friends practically compelled them to answer questions concerning their views about U.S. foreign policy and the so-called clash of civilizations between Islam and the West. Muslim Americans possessed a symbolic importance to the national culture that far outweighed their actual numbers. They became central figures in longstanding debates over what it meant to be an American.

When Keith Ellison, an African American Muslim, ran for and was elected to the U.S. Congress from Minnesota in 2006, he asked to borrow Thomas Jefferson's copy of the Qur'an, housed in the Library of Congress, for his swearing-in ceremony. Rather than carrying the Bible while reciting his oath of allegiance to the U.S. Constitution, Ellison wanted to bring his own sacred scripture. Conservative talk-show host Dennis Praeger called Ellison's decision "an act of hubris...that undermines American civilization." He said that those Americans "incapable" of taking an oath on the Bible should not serve in Congress.

In a similar vein, U.S. Representative Virgil Goode of Virginia used the controversy as an opportunity to attack liberal U.S. immigration policies, which he said would lead to "many more Muslims elected to office." Ignoring the fact that Ellison was an African American, Goode presented Muslims and Islam as foreign agents in America. He advocated the reduction of diversity visas and the virtual elimination of legal immigration from the Middle East. Otherwise, he argued, "we are leaving ourselves vulnerable to infiltration by those who want to mold the United States into the image of their religion, rather than working within the Judeo-Christian principles that have made us a beacon of freedom-loving persons around the world." Congressman Ellison ignored such criticism, and supported by a number of Americans, he carried Jefferson's copy of the Qur'an to his swearing-in ceremony.

As this incident showed, Muslim American life during the war on terrorism was open to the bright light of self-examination and vulnerable to the heat of prejudice. Commenting on this state of affairs, Iranian American literary scholar and poet Fatemeh Keshavarz pointed out that revolutionary and violent eras often produce hot, explosive rhetoric. Enemies see each other as caricatures, she observed. The ordinary, everyday moments of human life, laughter, and love wilt in such oppressive heat. "Perhaps what we need more than anything," she wrote in her literary memoir *Jasmine and Stars*, "is a global cooling that would allow us to look and listen." Keshavarz asserted that if we do listen to each other across the social and political lines that are supposed to divide us, there is the possibility that we might actually hear one another. "In the faint voices that reach us from across the globe," she almost whispered, "there is the recognition of our shared humanity. In laughing at the same joke, feeling the same pain, or admiring each other's work of art, there is an empowering flash of recognition."

The events of 9/11 threatened to silence such voices in Muslim America—or more accurately, made it impossible for some non-Muslim Americans to hear these voices. But if we listened closely enough, it was possible to sense the everyday, human realities of Muslim American life. One American journalist, for example, peeked behind the stereotypes of Muslims as religious fanatics and revealed what she called a "silent, secular majority of American Muslims." Reporting for the *New York Times*, Laurie Goodstein interviewed Khalid Pervaiz, an American Muslim investment banker from Los Angeles who considers himself a good Muslim despite the fact that he does not pray five times a day. "I don't think I'm less of a Muslim," he told Goodstein. "I'm just not a practicing, going-to-the-masjid Muslim."

Pervaiz, a South Asian American who attended a Roman Catholic school during his childhood in Lahore, Pakistan, said that he generally attended services at the mosque once a year for Eid al-Fitr, the holiday marking the end of the Ramadan fast. The father of two, Pervaiz sent his two daughters to Qur'an classes at the local mosque on Sundays. He also proudly displayed a Christmas wreath on his front door and put up a Christmas tree in his living room. Pervaiz was not alone. After 9/11, many other Muslims publicly identified themselves as secular Muslims, echoing the oft-heard phrase among Americans that they were "spiritual but not religious."

Of course, other Muslim Americans were proud to identify themselves as religious people, and proud to express their faith in ways that were as American as the flag and apple pie, as one journalist put it. Muslim Girl Scouts, for example, took a pledge to "serve Allah and my country, to help people and live by the Girl Scout Law." With several troops in cities and towns across the United States, the Muslim Girl Scouts blended specifically Islamic teachings with the generic goals of the Girl Scouts USA, the parent organization. Muslim Girl Scout troops sought to teach their members a strong sense of self-worth and independence, regard for other people's feelings and rights, a meaningful set of values, and a commitment to serving others.

For example, the Girl Scout troop associated with Atlanta Masjid of Islam went camping and learned how to make a fire, cook, and "live respectfully with the animals and Allah's creations." Working toward their Hunger 101 badge, troop members also volunteered at a local food bank. In New York, older scouts helped to clean up Prospect Park in Brooklyn. In addition to working toward the typical Girl Scout badges, Muslim scouts earned Islamic merit badges for answering questions about Islamic practices, for teaching non-Muslims about their religion, and for learning Islamic prayers. Like other troops, Muslim Girl Scouts also sold cookies and made s'mores. They wore the trademark brown and green clothing of Girl Scouts, but many scouts added the *hijab*, or head scarf, to their outfits.

Muslim scouts imbibed the American patriotism for which scouting is well-known. At a 2004 meeting at the Muslim Youth Center of Brooklyn, for example, scouts read and discussed a handbook entitled "Evolution of the Stars and Stripes." African American Muslim scout leader Stacey Salimah Bell taught a crowd of mainly Arab American Muslim scouts how to properly handle, fly, and fold the U.S. flag. One scout refused to say the pledge of allegiance to the flag, explaining that her only allegiance was to God. Bell affirmed that it was her personal choice, but gently encouraged the girl to consider her decision carefully. Most scouts at the Brooklyn Center did not see a contradiction between being patriotic and being pious. Marching in New York's Muslim Day Parade, they shouted, "M-U-S-L-I-M! We're so blessed to be with them! Girrrl Scouts! U-S-A! We're the hope of to-day."

In a similar way, members of Muslim Boy Scout troops formed after 9/11 said that the values of scouting echoed the values of Islam. In an interview with a journalist for *Time* magazine, one member of Houston's Troop 797 recited all twelve qualities of a good Boy Scout—he is trustworthy, loyal, helpful, friendly, courteous, kind, obedient, cheerful, thrifty, brave, clean, and reverent, concluding that "the values of scouting are so similar to what we learn in Islam." Like Muslim Girl Scouts, these Boy Scouts said that they were proud of being Americans. "I love my country," said one.

At the 2005 National Scout Jamboree, however, not all non-Muslim boy scouts were ready to accept Muslim scouts as equals. As Shemaz Hemani waited his turn at the jamboree's shooting range, a white boy teased him, asking, "What's up, Jihad?" Another Muslim scout was called "Saddam" by one of his peers. Bacon was served every morning at breakfast, and despite the fact that the troop had requested *halal* meals, there was no word about whether the salami lunchmeat contained pork. Fortunately, a Jewish patrol leader had brought along enough peanut butter and jelly to share with the Muslim scouts.

One other characteristic of Troop 797 stood out for at least some non-Muslims at the 2005 National Scout Jamboree. They were Isma'ili Muslims. The Isma'ilis are a branch of Shi'a Islam that split from other Muslims over the issue of which relative of the Prophet Muhammad should lead the Muslim community. They differ from most Shi'i Muslims in Iran, Iraq, Pakistan, and Lebanon in that they follow a different line of Imams, or Shi'i leaders. Thousands of Isma'ili Muslims immigrated to the United States after 1965 from South Asia and East Africa, often as political refugees. Among their number are some of the most prosperous and professionally successful Muslims in the United States.

Rather than going to mosques for their communal prayers, religiously observant Isma'ili Muslims gather two times a day, just before sunrise and during sunset, in *jama'atkhanas*, or meeting places. Like other Muslims, they wash before making their prayers and greet each other upon entering their shared religious space. Unlike many other Muslims, they also sing hymns and make food offerings as part of their religious ceremonies. Their prayers, which differ from the five daily prayers performed by many other Muslims, incorporate several verses from the Qur'an, and ask God's blessings on the Prophet Muhammad,

Ali, the family of the Prophet, and the current Imam, or leader, of the Isma'ili community. At the end of their prayers, they turn to the congregants next to them to shake hands and say, "May you glimpse the Lord's divine countenance!"

The presence of the Isma'ili troop at the Boy Scout Jamboree inspired one Mormon scout to proclaim that he never knew there were "lots of different kinds of Muslims." This lack of general knowledge of Islamic religious diversity was especially understandable after 9/11. As many academics, community activists, and media figures rushed to educate non-Muslims about the basic components of Islamic religion, Muslims and non-Muslims alike attempted to simplify it. Sometimes, they boiled it down to a few easily memorized set of beliefs that could be listed on a business card. Mosque information sessions, for example, often focused on the five pillars of Islamic practice, including the declaration of faith, daily prayers, charity, fasting during Ramadan, and the pilgrimage to Mecca. But the five pillars did not begin to encompass the diversity of Islamic religious activities in the United States, often ignoring Sufi, Shi'i, and other forms of Islamic religious expression.

What was needed, said many Muslim and non-Muslim Americans, was a deeper, more sustained interfaith movement among Americans. Though there were many interfaith discussions, circles, and organizations in the United States before 9/11, their importance to the public life of the nation increased in the years afterward. One of these noteworthy interfaith efforts was a popular cultural phenomenon called the Faith Club, created by Ranya Idliby, Suzanne Oliver, and Priscilla Warner. After 9/11, Palestinian Muslim American Ranya Idliby sought out two mothers, one Christian and one Jewish, to co-write a children's book about their three faiths' shared values. As these New York area mothers discussed the writing of the book, they discovered that they needed to understand one another's faiths better before writing the children's book together. They were bothered by their own stereotypes.

Meeting frequently, these three women confessed their own prejudices and discussed their most deeply held beliefs about the meaning of life, mortality, and faith. They agreed to be brutally honest and also compassionate with one another. Idliby, Oliver, and Warner read each other's personal journals and recorded their conversations. In 2006, they shared their story in a memoir called *The Faith Club*, a 320-page book that became a bestseller. They appeared on several popular TV and radio shows to promote the book, and they encouraged others to start their own faith clubs.

In addition to popular interfaith efforts such as the Faith Club, Muslim Americans supported interfaith dialogue among American religious leaders. The Islamic Society of North America (ISNA), for example, partnered with the Union for Reform Judaism (URF) to develop "Children of Abraham," a guide to interfaith conversations between Jews and Muslims. URF president Eric Yoffie and ISNA president Ingrid Mattson asserted that their faiths were historically intertwined and that their destiny was shared. Jews and Muslims must engage the hard issues, they said, including terrorism, Jerusalem, the Israeli-Palestinian conflict, and human rights. Jews and Muslims must also learn more about each others' traditions, they advised.

Muslim Americans also supported various international interfaith movements. In 2007, on the occasion of Eid al-Fitr, Muslim American leaders signed on to a communiqué from the world's Muslim leaders to the world's Christian leaders. Sponsored by the Royal Aal al-Bayt Institute for Islamic Thought in Amman, Jordan, "A Common Word between Us" outlined the scriptural, theological, and doctrinal bases in both Islamic and Christian traditions for peace between Christians and Muslims.

Signed by 138 Muslim leaders from around the world, the document inspired Yale University Divinity School to organize an interdenominational response from Christian leaders across the United States.

In the midst of these high level contacts, many Muslim Americans also stressed the need for more grassroots interfaith activism. Eboo Patel, the founder and executive director of Interfaith Youth Core, emphasized the imperative of involving children, adolescents, and young adults in interfaith activism. In his memoir, *Acts of Faiths*, he declared that "the shock troops of religious extremism were young people." Chronicling the adolescence of terrorists Yigal Amir, Eric Rudolph, and even a young Usama bin Ladin, Patel pointed out that "every time we read about a young person who kills in the name of God, we should recognize than an institution painstakingly recruited and trained that young person." Jews, Christian, and Muslims are not born terrorists. They are made. "If we had invested in our youth programs," Patel asked, "could we have gotten to those young people first?"

An Isma'ili American Muslim of Indian roots, Patel admitted that he understood the alienation that had led some young people into the schools and training camps of religious totalitarians. He grew up outside Chicago, where he experienced the pain of American racism. Like other alienated teenagers, he began acting out. In high school, however, YMCA youth programs directed his feelings of alienation toward service. First attracted to radical leftist politics as a college student at the University of Illinois, his service to a local nursery home, the Salvation Army, and a women's shelter led Patel toward a different notion of social justice. He became involved with a Catholic Workers house, which stressed communal living, service, and political activism all at the same time.

After graduating, Patel became a teacher at a Chicago alternative high school for dropouts and co-founded a utopian community called the Stone Soup Cooperative. Patel's co-founders became known as a community of young activists representing many faiths. At first, he struggled with this label—after all, he had never really felt deeply connected to his Islamic faith. But a trip to India, where he came to admire deeply his grandmother's service to others in the name of Islam, inspired in him a deep desire to engage his religious heritage. Patel won a Rhodes scholarship to study at Oxford University, and while there, he came to identify more strongly as a religious Muslim. For him, being Muslim meant taking a leap of faith, and it meant performing acts of faith that were consistent with Islam's "ethic of service and pluralism."

Eboo Patel sat out to create nothing less than an interfaith youth movement that was international in scope. In 1999, he met in the San Francisco Bay area with sixteen organizers from four different continents to establish the Interfaith Youth Core, which would rest on three pillars: "intercultural encounter, social action, and interfaith reflection." In various locales, young people of different faiths began to come together for community service projects. After September 11, 2001, Patel's vision suddenly became even more relevant and urgent. He sought and acquired funding from the Ford Foundation and local Chicago foundations. As he pitched his organization to various religious leaders, he encountered some resistance. How would kids participate in interfaith reflection when most of them did not understand the foundations of their own faiths?

Patel's answer was that the Interfaith Youth Core actually strengthened each person's knowledge of and commitment to his or her respective faith tradition. "We begin by identifying values that different religious communities hold in common—hospitality, cooperation, compassion, mercy. We bring a group of religious diverse young people together and ask them, 'How does your religion speak to this value?'" The result, explained Patel, was that youth were inspired to learn much more about their own faith so that they could explain their religious heritage to children of different religious backgrounds—all while performing community service projects together.

In 2003, the National Conference on Interfaith Youth Work met for the first time in Chicago. A national Day of Interfaith Youth Service was created, and Patel co-edited a book called *Building the Interfaith Youth Movement*. His Interfaith Youth Core became an important node in the growing transnational networks dedicated to interfaith youth activism. For Patel, this work expressed the pluralist vision that was at the core of his Islamic faith, the vision that social diversity itself was part of God's plan—that God made us different so that we might come to know each other and compete in goodness.

Was such a vision realistic in a post-9/11 world? The answer to that question depended as much, and probably more, on non-Muslims than on Muslims, at least in the United States. Muslim Americans could create all of the interfaith clubs they wanted, but non-Muslims would still have to join. U.S. government policies toward Muslims and Muslim-majority countries would likely shape the future of interfaith relations as much as any other factor. If another major terrorist incident occurred, worried Muslim Americans, how many of us would be rounded up for detention? Would I be fired from my job or attacked by an angry mob? Which Muslim-majority country would be invaded? How many would be killed? Such questions reflected the uneasy realities of Muslim American life after 9/11.

History taught Muslim Americans to be nervous about their status in the United States. But it also gave them a sense

115

of belonging. They have been part of America since before the republic was founded. Their contributions—some famous, some unknown—have changed the course of the nation's life. They contributed their labor to the nation's economic success in the nineteenth century. They produced some of the country's most memorable slave narratives. They served in the U.S. diplomatic corps and in the U.S. military. They published newspapers in the 1920s, created new forms of jazz in the 1950s, and changed the history of boxing and basketball. They built massive companies and massive buildings. They healed people, sang to them, and fed them. These historical memories suggested a different future for Muslims and non-Muslims in the United States, one that recognizes the inevitable interdependency of all Americans and offers the hope that understanding and compassion among us might yet prevail.

Despite the fact that Muslim American leaders unambiguously con-
demned terrorism after 9/11, many non-Muslim Americans in the
years following the tragedy asked Muslim Americans to clarify their
position. In 2005, the Fiqh Council of North America, a group of
prominent Muslim American scholars, issued a fatwa, *an authoritative*
interpretation of Islamic law and ethics, that explained why terrorism
is prohibited in Islam. Every major Muslim American organization
and more than 300 mosques and local Islamic groups endorsed it.

In the Name of God, the Compassionate, the Merciful.

The Fiqh Council of North America wishes to reaffirm Islam's
absolute condemnation of terrorism and religious extremism.

Islam strictly condemns religious extremism and the use of
violence against innocent lives.

There is no justification in Islam for extremism or terrorism.
Targeting civilians' life and property through suicide bombings
or any other method of attack is *haram*—or forbidden—and those
who commit these barbaric acts are criminals, not "martyrs."

The Qur'an, Islam's revealed text, states: "Whoever kills
a person [unjustly]...it is as though he has killed all mankind.
And whoever saves a life, it is as though he had saved all mankind" (5:32).

Prophet Muhammad said there is no excuse for committing
unjust acts: "Do not be people without minds of your own, saying that if others treat you well you will treat them well, and that
if they do wrong you will do wrong to them. Instead, accustom
yourselves to do good if people do good and not to do wrong
(even) if they do evil" (Al-Tirmidhi).

God mandates moderation in faith and in all aspects of life when He states in the Qur'an: "We made you to be a community of the middle way, so that (with the example of your lives) you might bear witness to the truth before all mankind" (2:143).

In another verse, God explains our duties as human beings when He says: "Let there arise from among you a band of people who invite to righteousness, and enjoin good and forbid evil" (3:104).

Islam teaches us to act in a caring manner to all of God's creation. The Prophet Muhammad, who is described in the Qur'an as "a mercy to the worlds" said: "All creation is the family of God, and the person most beloved by God (is the one) who is kind and caring toward His family."

In the light of the teachings of the Qur'an and Sunna we clearly and strongly state:

1. All acts of terrorism targeting civilians are *haram* (forbidden) in Islam.

2. It is *haram* for a Muslim to cooperate with any individual or group that is involved in any act of terrorism or violence.

3. It is the civic and religious duty of Muslims to cooperate with law enforcement authorities to protect the lives of all civilians.

We issue this fatwa following the guidance of our scripture, the Qur'an, and the teachings of our Prophet Muhammad— peace be upon him. We urge all people to resolve all conflicts in just and peaceful manners.

We pray for the defeat of extremism and terrorism. We pray for the safety and security of our country, the United States, and its people. We pray for the safety and security of all inhabitants of our planet. We pray that interfaith harmony and cooperation prevail both in the United States and all around the globe.

CHRONOLOGY

Sixteenth–nineteenth centuries
   Muslims from North and West Africa arrive in the Americas

1812
   Bilali Mahomet of Sapelo Island, Georgia, leads fellow slaves in preparing to fight the British during the war with Great Britain

1831
   Omar ibn Sayyid writes his autobiography in Arabic

1880s–World War I
   Muslim immigrants from the Ottoman Empire and South Asia arrive in the United States

1893
   Former U.S. consul Alexander Russell Webb, a white convert, represents Islam at the World Parliament of Religions in Chicago

1907
   Eastern European Muslims establish the American Mohameddan Society in New York

1910
   Inayat Khan, a Sufi Muslim musician from British India, tours the United States

1921
   Muhammad and Hussein Karoub build a Sunni mosque in Detroit, Michigan
   Muhammad Sadiq, missionary for the South Asian Ahmadiyya movement, begins publication of the *Moslem Sunrise* in Detroit, but establishes headquarters in Chicago the next year

1924

The National Origins Act further restricts immigration from non-European countries

1925

Noble Drew Ali, formerly Timothy Drew, establishes the Moorish Science Temple in Chicago

1926

Dusé Mohammed Ali and Kalil Bazzy establish the Universal Islamic Society in Detroit, uniting African Americans, Indians, and Arabs in one Sunni Muslim organization

1930

Wallace D. Fard, a mysterious peddler of unknown origins, creates the Nation of Islam in Detroit

1934

Fard disappears, and Elijah Muhammad, formerly Elijah Poole, claims leadership of the Nation of Islam

1937

Wali Akram founds the First Cleveland Mosque
Progressive Arabian Hashemite Society, a Shi'a mosque, is established in Detroit

Late 1930s

Muhammad Ezaldeen leads the Addeynu Allahe Universal Arabic Association

1939

Daoud Ahmed Faisal leases a building in New York for his Islamic Mission of America

1945

Albanian American Moslem Society formed in Detroit

1946

Malcolm Little is sent to prison, where he converts to the Nation of Islam

1952

Federation of Islamic Associations of the United States and Canada is created

1960s

Sufi Order of the West expands membership in the United States

Darul Islam, a Sunni Muslim movement, spreads among African Americans
Nation of Gods and Earths (the Five Percenters) formed in New York

1961

Muhammad Speaks newspaper begins publication and becomes a leading weekly in black America

1963

Foreign Muslim students create the Muslim Students Association at the University of Illinois

1964

Malcolm X breaks with Elijah Muhammad's Nation of Islam; goes on hajj to Mecca

1965

Malcolm X assassinated in New York; *Autobiography of Malcolm X* is published soon after
President Johnson signs the Hart-Celler Act, leading to increased immigration from Asia and Africa

1967

Muhammad Ali is stripped of his heavyweight boxing championship for refusing induction into the U.S. armed forces

1971

U.S. Supreme Court in a unanimous decision strikes down Muhammad Ali's conviction for refusing to serve in the armed forces

1973

Muslim Students Association officials establish the North American Islamic Trust

1975

Elijah Muhammad dies and his son W. D. Mohammed takes control of the Nation of Islam; initiates Sunni reformation of the movement
Alianza Islámica, a grassroots Latino/ American Muslim organization, is formed

1977–1978

Louis Farrakhan, former national spokesman for Elijah Muhammad, breaks with W. D. Mohammed and reconstitutes the Nation of Islam

1981–1982

Muslim Students Association forms the Islamic Society of North America, an umbrella group for the increasing number of Muslim professional and community organizations

1991

Siraj Wahhaj is the first Muslim to offer the invocation in the U.S. House of Representatives

1992

W. D. Mohammed is the first Muslim to give the invocation in the U.S. Senate

1994

Council of American-Islamic Relations (CAIR) is formed in Washington, D.C.

1995

Minister Louis Farrakhan leads the Million Man March

1996

Hillary Rodham Clinton hosts the first Eid al-Fitr, the festival marking the end of Ramadan, at the White House
U.S. Navy commissions a Muslim chaplain

2001

Members of al-Qa'ida murder approximately 3000 in coordinated attacks in New York and Washington
USA PATRIOT Act is signed into law

2003

United States invades Iraq

2006

Keith Ellison is the first Muslim elected to the U.S. Congress

2008

André Carson is the second Muslim elected to the U.S. Congress

FURTHER READING

GENERAL OVERVIEWS OF ISLAM IN
THE UNITED STATES

Curtis, Edward E. IV, ed. *Columbia Sourcebook of Muslims in the United States*. New York: Columbia University Press, 2008.

Haddad, Yvonne Yazbeck, and Jane Idleman Smith, eds. *Muslim Communities in North America*. Albany: State University of New York Press, 1994.

Smith, Jane I. *Islam in America*. New York: Columbia University Press, 1999.

AFRICAN AMERICAN MUSLIM SLAVES

Alford, Terry. *Prince Among Slaves: The True Story of an African Prince Sold Into Slavery in the American South*. New York: Oxford University Press, 2007.

Austin, Allan D. *African Muslims in Antebellum America: A Sourcebook*. New York: Garland, 1984.

Diouf, Sylviane A. *Servants of Allah: African Muslims Enslaved in the Americas*. New York: New York University Press, 1998.

Gomez, Michael A. *Black Crescent: The Experience and Legacy of African Muslims in the Americas*. New York: Cambridge University Press, 2005.

AMERICAN CONVERTS TO ISLAM

Abd-Allah, Umar F. *A Muslim in Victorian America: The Life of Alexander Russell Webb*. New York: Oxford University Press, 2006.

Clegg, Claude Andrew III. *An Original Man: The Life and Times of Elijah Muhammad.* New York: St. Martin's, 1997.

Curtis, Edward E. IV. *Black Muslim Religion in the Nation of Islam, 1960–1975.* Chapel Hill: University of North Carolina Press, 2006.

Dannin, Robert. *Black Pilgrimage to Islam.* New York: Oxford University Press, 2002.

McCloud, Aminah Beverly. *African American Islam.* New York: Routledge, 1995.

Turner, Richard Brent. *Islam in the African-American Experience*, 2d ed. Bloomington: Indiana University Press, 2003.

TWENTIETH-CENTURY MUSLIM IMMIGRANTS

Abraham, Nabeel, and Andrew Shryock, eds. *Arab Detroit: From Margin to Mainstream.* Detroit, MI: Wayne State University Press, 2000.

Bald, Vivek. "Overlapping Diasporas, Multiracial Lives: South Asian Muslims in U.S. Communities of Color, 1880–1950." *Souls* 8:4 (2006): 3–18.

Curtis, Edward E. IV. "Islamism and Its African American Muslim Critics: Black Muslims in the Era of the Arab Cold War." *American Quarterly* 59:3 (September 2007): 693–719.

Elkholy, Abdo. *The Arab Moslems in the United States.* New Haven, CT: College and University Press, 1966.

Haddad, Yvonne Y., and Jane I. Smith. *Mission to America: Five Islamic Sectarian Communities in North America.* Gainesville: University Press of Florida, 1993.

Lahaj, Mary. "The Islamic Center of New England." In *Muslim Communities in North America*, edited by Yvonne Yazbeck Haddad and Jane Idleman Smith, 293–315. Albany: State University of New York Press, 1994.

Sherman, William C., Paul L. Whitney, and John Guerrero. *Prairie Peddlers: The Syrian-Lebanese in North Dakota.* Bismarck, ND: University of Mary Press, 2002.

Trix, Frances. *The Albanians in Michigan*. East Lansing: Michigan State University Press, 2001.

Walbridge, Linda S. *Without Forgetting the Imam: Lebanese Shi'ism in an American Community*. Detroit, MI: Wayne State University Press, 1997.

RELIGIOUS AWAKENINGS OF THE LATE TWENTIETH CENTURY

Barboza, Steven. *American Jihad: Islam after Malcolm X*. New York: Doubleday, 1993.

Campo, Juan Eduardo. "Islam in California: Views from *The Minaret*." *Muslim World* 86: 3–4 (July–October 1996): 294–312.

Denny, Frederick Mathewson. "The Legacy of Fazlur Rahman." In *The Muslims of America*, edited by Yvonne Yazbeck Haddad, 96–108. New York: Oxford University Press, 1991.

Diaz, Idris M. "For the Love of Allah." *Philadelphia Inquirer Magazine*, April 2, 1989, 24–27, 30–36.

Haque, Amber, ed. *Muslims and Islamization in North America: Problems and Prospects*. Beltsville, MD: Amana Publications, 1999.

Hasan, Asma Gull. *American Muslims: The New Generation*. New York: Continuum, 2000.

Howell, Sally. "Finding the Straight Path: A Conversation with Mohsen and Lila Amen about Faith, Life, and Family in Dearborn." In *Arab Detroit: From Margin to Mainstream*, edited by Nabeel Abraham and Andrew Shryock, 243–54. Detroit, MI: Wayne State University Press, 2000.

Nimer, Mohammed. *The North American Muslim Resource Guide: Muslim Community Life in the United States and Canada*. New York: Routledge, 2002.

Rouse, Carolyn Moxley. *Engaged Surrender: African American Women and Islam*. Berkeley: University of California Press, 2004.

Wadud, Amina. *Qur'an and Woman: Rereading the Sacred Text from a Woman's Perspective*. New York: Oxford University Press, 1999.

Waugh, Earle H., and Frederick M. Denny, eds. *The Shaping of an American Islamic Discourse: A Memorial to Fazlur Rahman*. Atlanta: Scholars Press, 1998.

MUSLIM AMERICA AFTER 9/11

Al-Marayati, Laila. "American Muslim Charities: Easy Targets in the War on Terror." *Pace Law Review* 25 (2005): 321–38.

Chu, Jeff. "Duty, Honor, and Allah." *Time*, August 23, 2005.

Goodstein, Laurie. "Stereotyping Rankles Silent, Secular Majority of American Muslims." *New York Times*, December 23, 2001: A20.

Human Rights Watch. "We Are Not the Enemy: Hate Crimes against Arabs, Muslims and Those Perceived to be Arab or Muslim After September 11." Vol. 14, no. 6 (G), November 2002 (www.hrw.org/reports/2002/usahate/).

Idibly, Ranya, Suzanne Oliver, and Priscilla Warner. *The Faith Club: A Muslim, A Christian, A Jew—Three Women Search for Understanding*. New York: Free Press, 2006.

Jackson, Sherman A. *Islam and the Blackamerican: Looking toward the Third Resurrection*. New York: Oxford University Press, 2005.

Kassam, Tazim R. "The Daily Prayer (*Du'a*) of Shi'a Isma'ili Muslims." In *Religions of the United States in Practice*, vol. 2, edited by Colleen McDannell, 32–43. Princeton, NJ: Princeton University Press, 2001.

Keshavarz, Fatemeh. *Jasmine and Stars: Reading More than Lolita in Tehran*. Chapel Hill: University of North Carolina Press, 2007.

Patel, Eboo. *Acts of Faith: The Story of an American Muslim, The Struggle for the Soul of a Generation*. Boston: Beacon Press, 2007.

Pew Research Center. "Muslim Americans: Middle Class and Mostly Mainstream." Washington, D.C.: Pew Research Center, 2007.

Reinhertz, Shakina. *Women Called to the Path of Rumi: The Way of the Whirling Dervish*. Prescott, AZ: Homs Press, 2001.

Ulen, Eisa. "Girl Scouts: So Much More than Cookies." *Azizah* 3:2 (December 2003): 64–67.

Wolfe, Michael, ed. *Taking Back Islam: American Muslims Reclaim their Faith*. New York: Rodale, 2002.

INDEX

Abd al-Rahman Ibrahima
    abolitionists and, 9, 11
    capture and selling of, 6
    freedom of children, 8, 10
    Islamic practice of, 14–15
    "Oriental" identity of, 8–9
    requests for freedom, 7–8
    as slave, 7–9, 10, 11
    status in West Africa, 6, 7, 12
Abdallah, Mike, 48, 49
Abdullah, Aslam, 88
abolitionists, 9, 11
Acts of Faith (Patel), 113
Adams, John Quincy, 7
Addeynu Allahe Universal Arabic
    Association, 41–42
Afghanistan, 101
African American Muslims
    Muslim immigrants' lack of
        ties to, xi
    population of, 4
    religious imaginations of, 22
    slavery and, 11, 15, 44
    study of Qur'an, 78, 79–80
    on war on terrorism, 102
    women's religious lives, 17, 20

African American slaves
    African traditional religion
        and, 19, 20–21
    as Muslims, 4, 5, 14, 15,
        17–22, 116
African Americans
    Arab identity of, 41–42
    Arabic as original language of,
        32, 37, 43
    conversion of, 31–40
    economic independence of,
        43, 66
    Islam as original religion of,
        22, 37, 43
    migration from South to
        North, xiii, 31–32, 51
    Gamal Abdel Nasser as hero
        for, 62–63
    political self-determination of,
        33, 39, 43, 66
African traditional religion, 19,
    20–21
Ahmad, Ghulam, 26–27, 31, 37
Ahmadiyya movement
    Wali Akram and, 42–43
    Ahmad Din and, 33–34

Ahmadiyya movement (*continued*)
  English translation of Qur'an
    and, 34
  Nation of Islam compared
    to, 37
  Muhammad Sadiq and,
    31–33
  Sunni Islam and, 42–43
Akram, Wali, 42–43
Albania, 54–55, 60
Albanian American Moslem
    Society, 55, 60
Albanian Moslem Life, 55
Ali, Alef, 51
Ali, Noble Drew (Timothy
    Drew), 34–36, 41
All Dulles Area Muslim Society,
    98
All Moslem and Arab
    Convention (1943), 43
Allahabad Review, 27
Amana Growth Fund, 84
Amen, Lila, 89–90
Amen, Mohsen, 89–90
American Colonization Society,
    8, 12
American Islam
  American culture and, 59, 116
  chronology of, 119–22
  Hemlock Hill and, 41–42
  as international and cross-
    cultural, xii–xiii
  Moorish Science Temple and,
    34–36

religious awakenings in, 68–69,
    81, 83, 84, 86, 88, 91, 94
  See also African American
    Muslims; Muslim
    Americans; Muslim
    immigrants
American Islamic missions
  English translation of Qur'an
    and, 34
  Islamic Mission of America
    and, 40–41
  Inayat Khan and, 29–30
  Malcolm X as target of, 64, 66
  Moorish Science Temple
    and, 36
  Muslim Students Association
    and, 64
  Nation of Islam and, 36–40
  Muhammad Sadiq and, 31–33
  Shamin Siddiqui and, 90
  Sunni Islam and, 40–41
  Alexander Webb's
    establishment of, 27–29
  See also conversion to Islam
American Islamic Propaganda,
    28
American Moslem Society of
    Toledo, 57–60, 64
American Muslim Political
    Coordination Council,
    98–99
American Muslims (Hasan), 95–96
American patriotism
  Cold War and, 61

Islamic religious identity and, 57, 60
of Muslim Americans, 98
Muslim Girl Scouts and, 109
American values
Islam expressing, 28, 79
Islamic religious identity and, 58
Inayat Khan on, 30
mosques and, 57–58, 59, 60–61
Amir, Yigal, 113
Ancient Egyptian Arabic Order of the Nobles of the Mystic Shrine, 35
Arab American Banner Society, 67
Arab Americans
Federation of Islamic Associations and, 56–57
history of, 49–50
Islamic Mission of America and, 40
See also Muslim immigrants
Arab, Hajee Abdulla, 27
Arab identity, of African Americans, 41–42
Arabic language
Abd al-Rahman Ibrahima and, 6, 7, 9
Bilali and, 16
Ford Motor company employees and, 54
Job ben Solomon and, 2, 6
mosques' Arabic schools, 60
Muslim immigrants and, 48, 49, 53

Omar ibn Sayyid and, 12, 23
as original language of African Americans, 32, 37, 43
prayers in, 68
Ashcroft, John, 100
The Autobiography of Malcolm X (Malcolm X), 82
Azizah, 84
Azzam, Abd al-Rahman, 65

Baker, Ora Ray, 30
Bangladesh, 50–51, 73
Al-Bayan, 49
Beirut Marine barracks attack of 1983, 99
Bektashi order of Sufis, 56
Bell, Stacey Salimah, 109
ben Solomon, Job. See Job ben Solomon
Bengali Muslims, 50–52
Berber traders, 5
Bible, 12, 46
Bilali
Islamic practice of, 16–18, 19
as polygamist, 15
as slave, 15–16
Bilali, Salih, 20–21
bin Ladin, Usama, 80, 97, 113
Black Masons of Boston, 8
"Black Muslims." See Nation of Islam
Black on Both Sides (Mos Def), 101
Black Shriners, 35

Blavatsky, Helena, 26
Bluett, Thomas, 2
Blyden, Edward Wilmot, 33
Bosnia, 53
British merchant marine, 50
British Merchant Sailor's Club
    for Indian Seamen, 51
Brown, Katie, 17–19
Buddhism, 26
Buffalo Courier-Express, 41
Bush, George W., 99, 100, 101–2

Canada, 47, 49, 73
Caribbean, 73
Carlos Rivera Orchestra, 57
Chaudhary, Mohammad, 98
Cherry Hill Child Development
    Center, 92–93
Chicago World Fair of 1893,
    Parliament of Religions, 28
"Children of Abraham," 112
Chirri, Muhammad Jawad, 68
Choudry, Ibrahim, 51–52
Christian Messiah, 31, 37
Christian missionaries, 10–11,
    26, 33
Christianity
    Abd al-Rahman Ibrahima
        and, 9
    Job ben Solomon and, 2–3
    morality and, 90
    Omar ibn Sayyid and, 11–13, 23
    racism and, 32
    slaves converted to, 19

terrorism and, 113
    white, middle-class values and,
        58–59
*Christianity, Islam, and the Negro
    Race* (Blyden), 33
Christians for Peace and Justice
    in the Middle East, x
civil rights movement, 62
Clara Muhammad schools, 92
Clay, Henry, 7–8, 9
Cleveland, Grover, 27
Clinton, Bill, 103
Cold War, xiii, 61–62, 69
Columbus, Christopher, 4
conjure, 20
consumer products, 86
conversion to Islam
    adaptability of Islam and, 44
    Idris Diaz and, 82
    Ahmad Din and, 33–34
    Moorish Science Temple and,
        34–36
    Nation of Islam and, 36–40, 44
    political reasons for, 33, 43
    religious reasons for, 33, 44
    Muhammad Sadiq and, 31–33
    spouses of Muslim immigrants
        and, 52, 60
    Sunni Islam and, 40, 41
    Alexander Webb and, 25–29
    See also American Islamic
        missions
Council on American-Islamic
    Relations (CAIR), 94, 99

Couper, James Hamilton, 20–21

Cox, James Coates, 7

cultural integration, 57–58, 60

Daoud, Ouhnane, 103

Dar al-Islam (House of Islam), 67

dashiki, 84

dating, 80–81

Day of Interfaith Youth Service, 115

Def, Mos, 101–2

dhikr, 17, 56

Diaz, Idris M., 81–83

dietary rules, 2, 48, 52, 85–86

Din, Ahmad, 33–34, 42–43, 44, 45–46

Dodge Foundation, 57

Dow Jones Islamic Fund, 84

Dow Jones Islamic Market Indices, 84

Drew, Timothy, 34–36, 41

Druze, 53

Eddy, Mary Baker, 30

Edhi International Foundation, 98

Egypt, 61, 62–63

Eisenhower, Dwight D., 61, 62

Elkholy, Abdo, 57–58, 59, 60

Ellison, Keith, 106–7

Eminem, 102

equality
human equality, 28
social equality, 32

Estevanico, 4–5

The Eternal Message of Muhammad (Azzam), 65

Europe
imperial aggression of, 33
Muslim immigrants from, 47, 73

Everett, Edward, 8

Ezaldeen, Muhammad, 41, 43

Fadlallah, Muhammad Husayn, 89

Faisal, Daoud Ahmed, 40–41, 43, 66–67

Faith Club, 111–12

Fard, Wallace D., 36–37, 78, 79

Farrakhan, Louis, 79

Father Divine, 32

fatwas (religious opinions), 80, 117–18

Fauset, Arthur Huff, 36

Faysal (Saudi prince), 65

Federal Bureau of Investigation (FBI), 37–38, 100, 102–3

Federal Writers Project, 70

Federation of Islamic Associations (FIA), 56–57, 60, 68

Fiqh Council of North America, 117–18

First Cleveland Mosque, 43

First Fruit of the Druze, 53

flying back to Africa, 21–22

Ford Foundation, 114

Ford Motor company, 53–54
France, 62
Fruit of Islam, 39

Gallaudet, Thomas, 8
Garvey, Marcus, 32–33, 39, 43
Georgia Writers Project, 17
Gerner, Henry, x
Girl Scouts USA, 108
Goode, Virgil (U.S. Rep.), 106
Goodstein, Laurie, 107–8
Grace, Bishop Daddy, 32
Grand Mosque, Mecca, 82
Grant, Rachel, 21
Grant, Rosa, 20, 21
Grant, Ryna, 20, 21
Great Britain, 61, 62
Great Depression, 41–42
Great Migration, xiii, 31–32, 51
Gregg, Walter (Wali Akram),
    42–43
Griffin, Cyrus, 9
Guantanamo Bay, 105

Hadi, Sulaiman al-, 66
hadith, 11, 12, 74, 75
hajj, 40, 55, 64, 65, 81–83, 111
Hall, Shad, 17–18
*Handbook of Halaal and Haraam
    Products* (Uddin), 86
Hart-Celler Act of 1965, 72
Hasan, Asma Gull, 80–81, 95–96
Hashemite Hall, 54
hate crimes, 89, 94, 99–100

Hemani, Shemaz, 110
Hemlock Hill, 41–42
hijabs (head scarves), 18–19, 80,
    84, 100, 109
Hinduism, 26
*Holy Koran of the Moorish Science
    Temple* (Noble Drew Ali), 35
hoodoo, 20
Hoover, J. Edgar, 38
Hurricane Katrina, 101
Husayn, martyrdom of, 54, 56
Hussein, Saddam, 101

Ibn Sina, 73
Ibrahima, Abd al-Rahman.
    See Abd al-Rahman
    Ibrahima
Idliby, Ranya, 111–12
immigrants. *See* Muslim
    immigrants
Immortal Technique, 102
India, 50–52, 61, 73
Indianapolis International
    Airport, ix–xiv
Indonesia, 61
Institute for Islamic Research,
    Karachi, Pakistan, 73
interfaith marriages, 59–60
interfaith movements, 88, 110,
    111–15
Interfaith Youth Core,
    113–15
Internet, 80–81, 86
Iran, 61, 69, 73

Iranian Revolution of 1979, 88–90, 99
Iraq war of 1991, 97
Iraq war of 2003, 101
Islam
  adaptations of, 5, 44
  African traditional religion and, 19, 20–21
  American values and, 28, 79
  Edward Blyden on, 33
  ethical requirements of, 81, 86
  hoodoo and, 20
  internal disputes within, 31
  nineteenth-century American attitudes toward, 29
  as original religion of African Americans, 22, 37, 43
  post-9/11 criticism of, 104–5
  religious diversity and, 28, 56–57, 111
  social ethics of, 73, 74, 114
  twentieth-century American attitudes toward, 29
  as universal faith, 59
  in West Africa, 5–6, 18
  See also Ahmadiyya movement; American Islam; conversion to Islam
Islam and Modernity (Rahman), 75
Islam and World Peace (Muhaiyaddeen), 87–88
Islam in America (Webb), 28
Islamic Center of Geneva, 64, 66
Islamic Center of New England, 67–69
Islamic Center of Southern California, 88
Islamic Center of Toledo, 92
Islamic Center of Washington, D.C., 99
Islamic Dietary Laws and Practices, 86
Islamic feminist movement, 76, 77, 104, 105
Islamic Food and Nutrition Council of America, 86
Islamic Horizons, 85, 94
Islamic law
  alcoholic beverages and, 20, 58, 59, 68, 85
  Bilali and, 16
  dietary guidelines, 2, 48, 52, 85–86
  interpretations of Qur'an, 75
  investments and, 84
  Job ben Solomon and, 2
  marriage and, 75–76
  mortgages and, 67–68, 83
  Muslim Brothers and, 63
  Pakistan and, 90
  terrorism prohibited in, 117–18
Islamic Mahdi, 31, 37
Islamic Mission of America, 40–41
Islamic religious identity
  Islamic practice and, 1–2, 5, 14–21, 81–86, 91, 104

Islamic religious identity (*continued*)
  of Muslim Americans, 104,
    108
  of Muslim immigrants, 50, 52,
    55, 57–60, 69
  public advocacy of, 93–94
  styles of dress and, 84
Islamic schools, 92–93
Islamic Society of North America
    (ISNA), 91–94, 99, 104, 112
Islamists, 63, 74–75
Islamophobia, xiii
Isma'il, Vehbi, 55
Isma'ili Muslims, 110–11
Israel, 62, 69, 97

Jadakiss, 102
Jamaat-i Islami, 90
Jasmine and Stars (Keshavarz),
    107
Jefferson, Thomas, 106, 107
jellaba, 84
Jews
  ecumenical views of, 59
  interfaith movements and, 88,
    110, 111, 112, 113
  Omid Safi on, 105
  September 11, 2001, attacks
    and, 102
  See also Israel
jilbabs, 84–85
Job ben Solomon
  Arabic language and, 2, 6
  escapes of, 1–2

Islamic practice of, 1–2, 5,
    14–15
  as slave, xii, 1–2, 10
  status in West Africa, 2, 7
  travels of, xii, 2–4
Johnson, Lyndon B., 72
Johnson, P. Nathaniel. *See* Din,
    Ahmad
Jones, Charles Colcock, 19
Jones, Nero, 19
Juma, Charles, 48, 50, 71
Juma, Hassin, 47–48
Juma, Mary, 47–49, 50, 70–71

Ka'ba, 82, 83
Kadri, Chereffe, 92
Karoub, Hussein, 54
Karoub, Muhammad, 54
Keshavarz, Fatemeh, 107
Key, Francis Scott, 8, 12
Khadijah, 95–96
Khan, Ayyub, 74
Khan, Inayat, 29–30, 31, 44
Khan, Vilayat, 30
Khan, Zia, 30
Khomeini, Ayatollah, 88
KinderUSA, 103
Ku Klux Klan, 32
kuffiyeh, 84
kufi, 84
Kur, Budruddin, 27

Lebanon, 53, 54, 59, 67
Liberia, 33

Little, Earl, 39
Little, Louise, 39
Little, Malcolm. *See* Malcolm X
Lomax, James (Muhammad
    Ezaldeen), 41, 43

Madrid train bombings, March
    2004, 102
Mahbub, Hafis, 66–67
Mahony, Roger, 88
Malcolm X, 39, 63, 64–66, 79, 82
Mansa Musa (king of Mali), 5
Marayati, Laila al-, 103–4
marriage
    dating and, 81
    interfaith marriages, 59–60
    Islamic law and, 75–76
    mosques and, 55
    slave marriages, 15–16
Mattson, Ingrid, 104–5, 112
Mayfield, Brandon, 102–3
McCarran-Walter Act of 1952, 72
McKinnon, Everal, 70
Midamar, 85
Middle East, 62, 73, 97
Minaret, 88
Modern Age Arabian Islamic
    Society, 53
Mohammed, W. D., 78–79,
    83, 88
Montague, Duke of, 3
Moore, Francis, 3
Moorish Body Builder and Blood
    Purifier, 36

Moorish Mineral and Healing
    Oil, 36
Moorish Science Temple (MST),
    34–36, 38, 40, 41, 44
morality
    Muslim Americans and, 69, 81,
        88, 89–90
    Nation of Islam and, 38–39
Moslem Sunrise, 32, 34
The Moslem World, 28
Mosque No. 7, 64
mosques
    Wali Akram and, 43
    American values and, 57–58,
        59, 60–61
    architecture of, 91–92
    Louis Farrakhan and, 79
    financing of, 67–68
    Grand Mosque, Mecca, 82
    growth of, 91, 93
    information sessions and, 111
    interfaith marriages and,
        59–60
    Islamic Mission of America,
        40–41
    Islamic religious identity and,
        55, 57, 60
    leadership structure of, 92
    Elijah Muhammad and, 64
    Muslim immigrants and,
        48–49, 53, 54, 55–61, 68, 71
    Muslim Students Association
        and, 64
    Nation of Islam and, 64, 78, 79

mosques (*continued*)
North American Islamic Trust and, 84
Shi'a Islam, 54
Sunni Islam, 54, 55–56
Amina Wadud leading prayers and, 77, 104
in West Africa, 5
Mossadeq, Mohammed, 61
Mother Mosque of America, 53
Muhaiyaddeen, M. R. Bawa, 87–88
Muhammad (Prophet of Islam)
Ahmad Din on, 34, 45
hadith, 74, 75
Muslim Brothers and, 63
Qur'an revealed to, 34, 40, 45
as seal of the prophets, 31
Shi'a Islam and, 54
See also Sunna
Muhammad, Clara, 38, 92
Muhammad, Ebn, 41
Muhammad, Elijah
black political self-determination and, 39, 83
FBI and, 37–38
Islamic schools and, 92
as Messenger of God, 37, 78, 79
Gamal Abdel Nasser and, 62–63
unorthodox teachings of, 37, 64, 82
Muhammad, Farad, 36–37, 78, 79

Muhammad Speaks, 82
Muhammad, Wallace D. *See* Mohammed, W. D.
Musharraf, Pervez, 105
Muslim Americans
dietary rules and, 85–86
different life experiences of, xi, xii, xiv
hajj and, 81, 82–83
hate crimes against, 89, 94, 99–100
interfaith activism of, 113–15
Iranian revolution of 1979 and, 88–90
Islamic practice and, 81–86, 91, 104
Islamic schools of, 92–93
morality and, 69, 81, 88, 89–90
Muslim immigrants' relationship with, xii, 67
political activism after 9/11, 104
prosecuted as terrorists, 102–3
Qur'an and, 77, 79, 80, 81, 85, 86, 89, 95–96
racial segregation and, xii
Fazlur Rahman and, 75, 76, 77
reaction to 9/11 attacks, 97–99
recognition as authentic interpreters of Islam, 104–5
Shamin Siddiqui and, 90–91
silent, secular majority of, 107–8
status in America, 115–16
styles of dress, 84–85

Sufism and, 86–88
suspected of terrorism, 100, 105
on terrorism, 98–99, 117
U.S. foreign policy and, xiii,
    61–62, 69, 106
Amina Wadud and, 76, 77
on war on terrorism, 102
Muslim Boy Scouts, 109–11
Muslim Brothers, 63–64
Muslim Council Center, 98
Muslim Day Parade, 109
Muslim Girl Scouts, 108–9
Muslim Girls Training-General
    Civilization Class, 38–39
Muslim immigrants
    from Albania, 54–55, 60
    Arab American Banner Society
        and, 68
    diversity of, xii, 56–57, 68–69
    Ford Motor company and,
        53–54
    Hart-Celler Act and, 73
    from India, 50–52
    Islamic Mission of America
        and, 40
    Islamic religious identity and,
        50, 52, 55, 57–60, 69
    Islam's religious rules and,
        67, 68
    Malcolm X and, 66
    as Muslim American leaders,
        xi, 68
    Muslim Americans'
        relationship with, xii, 67

percentage of, 73
as political refugees, 110
post-9/11 immigration policies
    and, 106–7
racial segregation and, xii
religious awakenings and, 68–69
religious institutions
    established by, 53
    schools of, 92
    from Syria, 47–48, 53, 54, 59,
        67, 70–71
U.S. foreign policy and, 61, 63
The Muslim Journal, 85
Muslim Public Affairs Council,
    80–81, 99
Muslim Students Association, 63,
    83–84, 93, 98
Muslim Women's League, 103
Muslim Youth Center, Brooklyn,
    109
mutual aid societies, 53, 54

Nasser, Gamal Abdel, 61, 62–63
Nation of Islam
    conversion to Islam and,
        36–40, 44
    Wallace D. Fard establishing,
        36–37
    Louis Farrakhan and, 79
    Malcolm X and, 39, 79
    W. D. Mohammed as leader
        of, 78–79
    Elijah Muhammad as leader
        of, 37–38, 39, 78

Nation of Islam (*continued*)
   Gamal Abdel Nasser and, 63
   teachings of, 64, 82
   women in, 38–39
National Conference on
   Interfaith Youth Work, 115
National Origins Act of 1924,
   xiii, 55, 72
National Scout Jamboree, 110, 111
Nehru, Jawaharlal, 61
New Thought, 35
New York Times, 29
niqabs, 84–85
North Africa, 5, 73
North American Islamic Trust,
   83–86

Oglethorpe, James, 2
Olcott, Henry Steel, 26
Oliver, Suzanne, 111–12
Omar ibn Sayyid
   autobiography of, 13–14, 23–24
   Christianity and, 11–13, 23
   Islamic practice of, 14–15
   Qur'an and, 11, 12, 13, 16, 23
   as slave, 11–12, 14
OPEC oil embargo, 99
"Oriental" identity, 8–9
"Oriental" religions, 26, 31
Osman, Ahmed, 64
Owen, Jim, 12, 14, 24

Pace Law Review, 103
Pakistan, 73, 74, 90, 105

Pakistan League of America, 52
Palestinian refugees, 62, 63
pan-Africanism, 66
Patel, Eboo, 113–15
Peace Mission movement, 32
Persian Gulf, 97
Pervaiz, Khalid, 107–8
polygamy, 15, 75–76
Poole, Elijah. *See* Muhammad,
   Elijah
popular culture, 88
Praeger, Dennis, 88, 106
prayer
   Abd al-Rahman Ibrahima and, 9
   African American slaves and,
      20, 21–22
   in Arabic language, 68
   Bilali and, 17, 19
   flying back to Africa and, 21–22
   in Islamic practice, 17, 19, 20,
      21, 81, 110–11
   Job ben Solomon and, 1–2
   Nero Jones and, 19
   Omar ibn Sayyid and, 12, 14
   Amina Wadud and, 77, 104
   washing before daily prayers,
      ix–xiv

Qadiri Sufi order, 18, 87
al-Qa'ida, 80, 97, 101
Qur'an
   Abd al-Rahman Ibrahima and, 9
   amulets containing passages
      of, 21

Bilali and, 16
conversion to Islam and, 44
on differences in peoples, xi
Ahmad Din on, 34, 45–46
Muhammad Ezaldeen and, 41
Internet and, 80–81
Isma'ili Muslims and, 110
Thomas Jefferson's copy of,
   106, 107
Job ben Solomon and, 2–3
literacy and, 77–78
Hafis Mahbub as teacher of, 66
W. D. Mohammed and, 79
moral solutions of, 74
Muslim Americans and,
   77, 79, 80, 81, 85, 86, 89,
   95–96
Muslim Brothers and, 63
Omar ibn Sayyid and, 11, 12,
   13, 16, 23
as oral and aural text, 78
polygamy and, 75–76
Qadiri Sufi order and, 87
Fazlur Rahman and, 74–76, 81
Sunni Islam and, 40
on terrorism, 117
Amina Wadud on, 76, 81
women's study of, 79–80
Qur'an and Woman (Wadud),
   76, 77

racial segregation, xii
racism
   Christian racism, 32

Islamic religion as political
   solution to, 66–67
Malcolm X and, 65–66
Eboo Patel on, 113
separation of races as solution
   to, 39
Rahman, Fazlur, 73–76, 77, 81
Rahman, Mahfouz, 82–83
Ramadan, 20, 40, 48, 52, 55, 81,
   108, 111
Ramadan, Said, 66
Rexheb, Baba, 56
Roosevelt, Franklin D., 17
Roque, Frank, 99–100
Ross, North Dakota, 47–50
Rouse, Carolyn, 79–80
Royal Aal al-Bayt Institute
   for Islamic Thought, 112–13
Royal African Company, 3
Rudolph, Eric, 113

Sadiq, Muhammad, 31–33
Safi, Omid, 105
St. Simons Island, Georgia, 15
Salaam, Ishaq, 83
Sapelo Island, Georgia, 15–19
Saud (king of Saudi Arabia), 67
Saudi Arabia, 63, 69, 105
Sayyed, Tahleeb, 42
September 11, 2001, attacks
   backlash against Muslim
   Americans, 99–100
   criticism of Islam following,
   104–5

September 11, 2001 (*continued*)
  interfaith movements and, 111–15
  Islamic Center of Toledo and, 92
  Muslim American reactions to, 97–98
  Muslim Americans' political activism after, 104
  U.S. foreign policy and, 97, 101, 105, 106
  war on terrorism and, 101–2, 106, 107
shalwar kameez, 84
shari'a. See Islamic law
Shawarbi, Mahmoud Youssef, 64–65
Shi'a Islam
  diversity of Islamic religious activities and, 111
  Husayn's martyrdom and, 54, 56
  Isma'ili Muslims and, 110
  morality and, 88, 89
  mosques of, 54
Siddiqui, Shamim, 90–91
Sisters in Islam, 77
slave marriages, 15–16
slave religion
  African American slaves as Muslims, 4, 5, 14, 15, 17–22, 116
  African traditional religion, 19, 20–21
  clandestine nature of, 14

slavery
  Abd al-Rahman Ibrahima on, 9–10
  African American Muslims and, 11, 15, 44
  Bilali and, 15–16
  Omar ibn Sayyid and, 11–12, 14
  transatlantic slave trade, xiii, 1, 5, 6
Smith, Dante, 101
social justice, 88–89
Sodhi, Balbir Singh, 99–100
South America, 73
South Asia, 50
South Vietnam, 69
Southeast Asia, 73
Soviet Union, 61, 62
Spaulding, Thomas, 15
spiritualism, 26
State Street Mosque, Brooklyn, New York, 66
The Status of Muslim Civil Rights in the United States (Council on American-Islamic Relations), 94
Stone Soup Cooperative, 114
sub-Saharan Africa, 73
Subway sandwich shops, 85
Suez Canal, 62
Sufi Muslims
  Bilali as, 18
  diversity of Islamic activities and, 111

growth in, 86–88
Inayat Khan and, 29–30, 31, 44
lodges of, 55–56
Sufi Order International, 30
Sufi Ruhaniat International, 30
Sukarno, 61
Sunna
    Bilali and, 16
    Internet as discussion forum
        and, 80–81
    W. D. Mohammed and, 79
    Muslim Americans' study of,
        78
    Muslim Brothers and, 63
    terrorism and, 118
Sunni Islam
    as adaptation of Islamic
        tradition, 44
    Addeynu Allahe Universal
        Arabic Association and,
        41–42
    Ahmadiyya movement and,
        42–43
    American Islamic mission and,
        40–41
    Idris Diaz and, 82
    Malcolm X and, 39, 64–65
    W. D. Mohammed and, 79
    morality and, 88
    mosques, 54, 55–56
    Nation of Islam and, 78
    Ishaq Salaam and, 83
Syria, Muslim immigrants from,
        47–48, 53, 54, 59, 67, 70–71

Taliban regime, in Afghanistan,
        101
Tappan, Arthur, 8
Tappan, Charles, 8
tarboosh, 84
Taylor, John Louis, 12
Teasley, Mary, 76
tekke, 55–56
terrorism
    Christianity and, 113
    fatwa against, 117–18
    Muslim Americans on, 98–99,
        117
    Muslim Americans prosecuted
        as terrorists, 102–3
    Muslim Americans suspected
        of, 100, 105
    Muslim charities targeted as
        supporters of, 103
    war on, 101–2, 106, 107
theosophy, 26, 28, 35
thobe, 84
Time magazine, 109
Torah, 45
transatlantic slave trade, xiii, 1,
        5, 6
Truman, Harry S,
        61
Turkey, 73
Turner, Nat, 11

Uddin, Zaheer, 86
Ullah, Habib, 51–52
umma, 104

Union for Reform Judaism (URF), 112
Uniting Islamic Societies of America, 43
Universal House of Prayer for All People, 32
Universal Negro Improvement Association (UNIA), 32–33, 39
University of Islam, 78, 92
U.S. Commission on International Religious Freedom, 103
U.S. foreign policy
  Cold War and, xiii, 61–62, 69
  September 11, 2001, attacks and, 97, 101, 105, 106
U.S. government
  human rights abuses at Guantanamo Bay, 105
  mixed messages concerning Muslim Americans, 100, 104, 115
U.S. Justice Department, 103
U.S. Treasury Department, 103
USA Patriot Act, 100

Van Buren, Martin, 25
Vedas, 45–46
violence, criticism of, 104, 105

Wadud, Amina, 76–77, 81, 104
Walker, David, 8
Warner, Priscilla, 111–12

Webb, Alexander Russell, 25–29, 31, 35
West Africa
  Islam in, 5–6, 18
  transatlantic slave trade and, 1, 5, 6
white, middle-class Americans, 28–29, 58–59, 60
white supremacy, 43
women
  American Moslem Society and, 60
  Muhammad Ezaldeen and, 41
  Asma Gull Hasan on, 95–96
  hijabs and, 18–19, 80, 84, 100, 109
  Islamic feminist movement, 76, 77
  in Nation of Islam, 38–39
  religious lives of, 17, 20
  role as leaders, 92, 104–5
  study of Qur'an, 79–80
  Amina Wadud on, 76, 104
Works Projects Administration (WPA), 17, 70
World Community of al-Islam in the West, 79
World Muslim League, 65
World War II, 42, 50

Yale University Divinity School, 113
YMCA, 113
Yoffie, Eric, 112

ACKNOWLEDGMENTS

It may be a short book, but the list of people who helped me write it is long. Two anonymous readers for the Press gave constructive criticism in response to my proposal for the book. Jon Butler and Skip Stout, series editors, read the entire manuscript and offered wise counsel and collegial support throughout the entire process. Indiana University–Purdue University Indianapolis (IUPUI) Department of Religious Studies colleagues David Craig, Philip Goff, Kelly Hayes, Bill Jackson, Ted Mullen, Sonja Spear, Peter Thuesen, and Rachel Wheeler gave me excellent feedback on chapters 1, 3, and 4. Regan Zwald helped me tell a better story in chapter 1. Kathryn Lofton made useful suggestions for improvement on chapters 2 and 3. Four anonymous reviewers, colleagues who are experts in some aspect of Islam in America, offered both praise and criticism of the book's first complete draft, and I am very thankful to them for helping me make the final draft better.

Oxford University Press executive editor Nancy Toff generously edited each line of the book and strengthened the work's style and substance by asking tough questions and offering wonderful suggestions. She is a gift to the publishing industry.

The School of Liberal Arts at IUPUI, as always, gave me strong institutional support, and I am especially grateful to former dean Robert White, Bill and Gail Plater, and all those who have been instrumental in making it possible for me to work in such a collegial place.

I want to thank the Carnegie Corporation of New York whose 2008 Carnegie Scholar's grant made it possible for me to take leave and complete this work in a timely fashion. Needless to say, the views expressed in this work are solely the responsibility of the author. For some years now, Carnegie Scholars program director Patricia Rosenfield has encouraged me to pursue new lines of inquiry in the study of Islam in America, and I truly appreciate her enthusiasm for my work.

While the scholarly literature on Muslim Americans listed in the further reading section was essential to the book's overarching themes and ideas, primary sources allowed me to narrate the human stories at the heart of this book. Slave narratives, Works Project Administration interviews, ethnographic accounts, government documents, poems, songs, sermons, memoirs, Muslim American periodicals, and other first-person accounts provided the details of everyday life in Muslim America. I thank the many librarians who helped me to obtain those sources, especially the interlibrary loan staff at the IUPUI University Library.

I am grateful to those rights holders who gave permission to reprint portions of their works for the source documents in each chapter. Thanks to Asma Gull Hasan, Dr. Muzammil Siddiqi of the Fiqh Council of North America, and the American Historical Association. Thanks also go to Mouhamad Alloosh, Imad Ardah, Carrie Foote, Rabia Jermoumi, and Maryam Khan.

My son, Zayd, is too young yet to read this book, and while I am proud to dedicate it to him, I am even prouder that the writing of it did not keep me away from him too much.

TEXT CREDITS

Omar ibn Sayyid, "The Autobiography of Omar ibn Sayyid" (1831), edited by John Franklin Jameson, *American Historical Review* 30, no. 4 (July 1925): 791–95. Reprinted by permission of the American Historical Association.

Sheik Ahmad Din, "Living Flora—And Dead," *Moslem Sunrise* (January 1924): 14–15.

Interview with Mary Juma, Works Progress Administration, North Dakota Writers' Project, Ethnic Group Files, Series 30559, Roll 3, 1939.

Asma Gull Hasan, *American Muslims: The Next Generation* (New York: Continuum, 2000), 107–8. Reprinted by permission of Asma Gull Hassan.

Muzammil Siddiqi, chair, Fiqh Council of North America, "Fatwa against Terrorism," 2005. Reprinted by permission of Muzammil Siddiqi.

ART CREDITS

ABOUT THE AUTHOR

Edward E. Curtis IV is Millennium Chair of the Liberal Arts and Professor of Religious Studies at Indiana University-Purdue University Indianapolis (IUPUI). He is the author of *Black Muslim Religion in the Nation of Islam, 1960–1975* and *Islam in Black America* and the editor of *The Columbia Sourcebook of Muslims in the United States* and the *Encyclopedia of Muslim-American History*.